Southern Living®

ALL-TIME FAVORITE

PASTA
RECIPES

D1305200

Southern Living®

ALL-TIME FAVORITE
PASTA
RECIPES

Compiled and Edited by
Jean Wickstrom Liles

Oxmoor
House®

Copyright 1996 by Oxmoor House, Inc.
Book Division of Southern Progress Corporation
P.O. Box 2463, Birmingham, Alabama 35201

All rights reserved. No part of this book may be reproduced in any
form or by any means without the prior written permission of the
Publisher, excepting brief quotes in connection with reviews written
specifically for inclusion in a magazine or newspaper.

Library of Congress Catalog Number: 96-67712
Hardcover ISBN: 0-8487-2231-0
Softcover ISBN: 0-8487-2224-8
Manufactured in the United States of America
First Printing 1996

Editor-in-Chief: Nancy Fitzpatrick Wyatt
Editorial Director, Special Interest Publications: Ann H. Harvey
Senior Foods Editor: Susan Carlisle Payne
Senior Editor, Editorial Services: Olivia Kindig Wells
Art Director: James Boone

Southern Living® ALL-TIME FAVORITE PASTA RECIPES

Menu and Recipe Consultant: Jean Wickstrom Liles
Assistant Editor: Kelly Hooper Troiano
Copy Editor: Jane Phares
Editorial Assistant: Valorie J. Cooper
Indexer: Mary Ann Laurens
Concept Designer: Melissa Jones Clark
Designer: Rita Yerby
Senior Photographers: Jim Bathie; Charles Walton IV, *Southern Living* magazine
Photographers: Ralph Anderson; Tina Evans, J. Savage Gibson, Sylvia Martin, *Southern Living* magazine
Senior Photo Stylists: Kay E. Clarke; Leslie Byars Simpson, *Southern Living* magazine
Photo Stylist: Virginia R. Cravens
Production and Distribution Director: Phillip Lee
Associate Production Managers: Theresa L. Beste, Vanessa D. Cobbs
Production Coordinator: Marianne Jordan Wilson
Production Assistant: Valerie L. Heard

Our appreciation to the editorial staff of *Southern Living* magazine and to the Southern Progress Corporation
library staff for their contributions to this volume.

Cover: Pasta Stuffed with Five Cheeses (recipe on page 89)
Page 1: Super-Quick Pasta (recipe on page 77)
Page 2 : Tri-Colored Fettuccine Alfredo (recipe on page 95)

Contents

Pasta Primer

Bring on the pasta! For versatility and ease of preparation, pasta is hard to beat.
It is healthy and fits any budget. It can serve one or two or a crowd.
A meal built on a base of pasta can be casual or elegant, leisurely or quick.
From alphabets to ziti, there is a pasta to please almost every palate.

Pasta—What's Available

Pasta, available in a variety of shapes, sizes, and flavors, may be dried or fresh. However, the nutritional value of all the types is about the same.

Dried pasta is a favorite because it is inexpensive and has a long shelf life. Fresh pasta is made with eggs and flour and cooks a bit more quickly than the dried pasta. Look for fresh pasta in the refrigerated section at the supermarket, or follow our step-by-step instructions beginning on page 10 to make your own.

In Shape with Pasta

Choose a pasta shape and sauce that complement each other. To help identify the many shapes of pasta, use the Guide to Pasta on pages 8 and 9.

Long Shapes. Spaghetti, fettuccine, linguine, and angel hair are the most popular and versatile. Team thick strands with heavy, hearty sauces and thin strands with light, delicate sauces.

Medium Shapes. Penne, ziti, rigatoni, and mostaccioli (all tubular shapes) have holes and ridges and pair well with chunky, hearty sauces. Bow ties, elbow macaroni, radiatore (fat, rippled pasta), wagon wheels, and medium shells are popular in salads, casseroles, and stews.

Small Shapes. Ditalini (small tubular pasta), orzo (rice-shaped pasta), and alphabets are suited for soups, salads, and sauces with small chopped vegetables.

Egg Noodles. Available in fine, medium, wide, and extra wide, these are commonly used in casseroles and soups. As the name implies, egg noodles contain egg; most other dry pastas do not.

Specialty Shapes. Lasagna, manicotti, and jumbo shells are almost always used in baked dishes. Ravioli and tortellini are filled with meat, cheese, or other ingredients.

Perfect Pasta Every Time

• Cook pasta in a pasta pot with a removable perforated inner basket, or create one using a large Dutch oven or stockpot with a colander or large wire basket placed inside. The pasta needs plenty of room to bubble in boiling water. To drain, lift the basket, and shake off excess water.

• Use 4 to 6 quarts of water to cook 1 pound of dried pasta. Add pasta gradually to rapidly boiling water so that the water never stops boiling. (A rapid boil means the water is bubbling and moving around swiftly.) After all pasta has been added, stir once, and begin timing.

• Add salt and 1 teaspoon oil to boiling water, if desired. The oil helps keep the pasta from sticking; however, too much oil will cause the sauce to slide off the pasta. If you do not add oil, stir pasta frequently to prevent sticking.

• Cooking times vary with the size, shape, and moisture content of the pasta. Dried pasta cooks in 4 to 15 minutes, while refrigerated pasta requires only 2 to 3 minutes. Follow package directions. Begin checking pasta for doneness 1 minute before its minimum cooking time. Remove a piece of pasta from the water, and cut a bite from it. It is ready when it is al dente ("to the tooth" in Italian)—firm but tender, chewy not soggy.

• If the pasta is to be used in a dish that requires further cooking, slightly undercook the pasta.

• Drain pasta immediately. If pasta is to be reheated or chilled, rinse under cold water to stop the cooking process and to remove excess starch.

• Rinse under running water pasta that sticks together. For warm pasta dishes, use hot water, and for cold pasta dishes use cold water.

• Save a small amount of the hot cooking liquid to toss with the pasta if it seems too dry.

• Get a head start on a future meal by cooking a little extra. To store cooked pasta, toss lightly with 1 to 2 teaspoons vegetable oil to prevent sticking. Cover and chill up to 4 days, or freeze up to 6 months.

• To reheat cooked pasta, place it in a colander, and run hot water over it. Or drop the pasta in boiling water, let stand for 1 to 2 minutes, and then drain.

Interchanging Pasta Shapes

Give pasta dishes a new twist by using a different shape pasta. It is best to substitute a pasta that is similar in size and thickness to the one called for in the recipe. Here are some pastas that may be interchanged:

• Spaghetti, Thin Spaghetti, or Linguine
• Vermicelli, Thin Spaghetti, or Angel Hair
• Radiatore or Elbow Macaroni
• Wagon Wheels or Elbow Macaroni
• Elbow Macaroni or Medium Shells
• Mostaccioli, Penne, or Ziti
• Rotini or Ziti
• Bow Ties or Rigatoni
• Bow Ties or Ziti
• Orzo, Alphabets, or Ditalini

Pasta Measures Up

Uncooked pasta of similar sizes and shapes may be interchanged in recipes if it is measured by weight, not volume. Cooked pasta, however, should be substituted cup for cup. In general, allow 1 to 2 ounces of uncooked pasta or ½ to 1 cup cooked pasta per person.

Linguine, Spaghetti, or Vermicelli:
    4 ounces dry = 2 to 3 cups cooked
    8 ounces dry = 4 to 5 cups cooked
    16 ounces dry = 8 to 9 cups cooked

Macaroni, Penne, Rotini, or Shells:
    4 ounces dry = 2½ cups cooked
    8 ounces dry = 4½ cups cooked

Fine or Medium Egg Noodles:
    4 ounces dry = 2 to 3 cups cooked
    8 ounces dry = 4 to 5 cups cooked

Guide to Pasta . . .

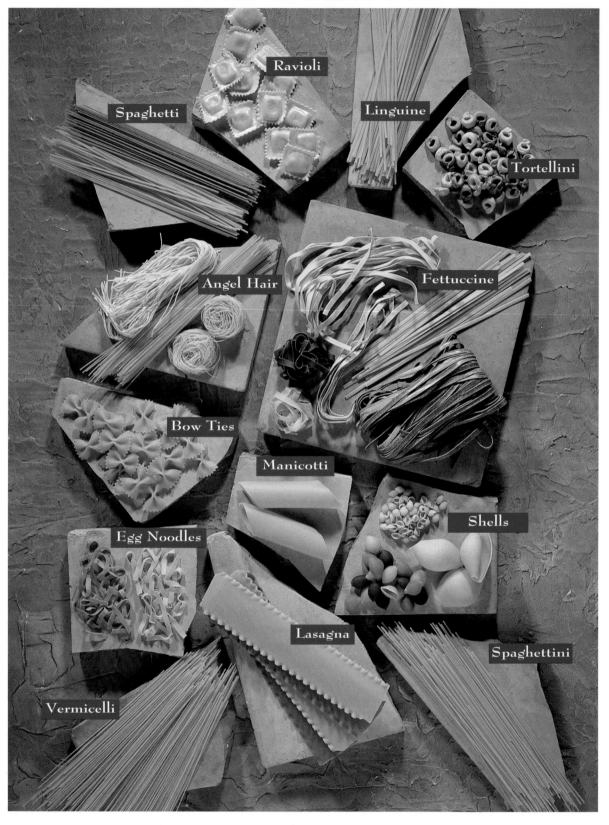

Ravioli

Spaghetti

Linguine

Tortellini

Angel Hair

Fettuccine

Bow Ties

Manicotti

Shells

Egg Noodles

Lasagna

Spaghettini

Vermicelli

. . . from A to Z

Tripolini

Raviolini

Gemelli

Ditalini

Rotini

Macaroni

Rigatoni

Fusilli

Cavatappi

Gnocchi

Ziti

Wagon Wheels

Pastina

Orzo

Penne

Radiatore

Make Your Own Pasta

If you enjoy pasta, you can double the enjoyment by making your own. The procedure takes some practice, but once you get the knack, it is simple and fun. And pasta purists maintain that there is a world of difference in terms of flavor and texture between the homemade and purchased varieties.

The differences between brands of flour account for the wide range in flour and water amounts called for in our recipe. Start with the minimum amount of flour and water; if the dough seems too dry, add a few more drops of water. If too sticky, knead in a little extra flour. The dough should be firm at the beginning. It will soften as it is kneaded and worked through the pasta machine or rolled out by hand.

Work with the dough, and give it a chance to soften before you add extra water. Otherwise, you might have to add more flour later. Experience is the best guide to knowing when the dough is the right consistency.

Roll the dough in a pasta rolling machine, or roll it out by hand. Most pasta machines have attachments for quickly cutting strips of rolled dough into different widths. You may also use a fluted-edged pastry wheel, a plain-edged roller, a pizza cutter, or a sharp knife with a thin blade to cut the dough into strips.

If you make your own ravioli (see page 12 for recipe), you may want to use a special ravioli rolling pin.

Allow cut pasta to dry 15 to 30 minutes before cooking. Hang it over a wooden drying rack, or spread it out on a kitchen towel to dry. Handle with care; freshly made pasta dough is delicate.

Homemade pasta cooks faster than commercial pasta (in just 1 to 2 minutes). To cook, add fresh pasta to boiling water with salt and a small amount of oil to keep it from sticking.

Homemade Pasta

3 large eggs
3 to 4 cups all-purpose flour
1 teaspoon salt
2 to 4 tablespoons water
3 quarts boiling water
1 teaspoon salt
1 tablespoon olive oil

Beat eggs in a large mixing bowl, using a wire whisk. Add one-fourth of flour and 1 teaspoon salt; beat with a wire whisk until blended. Work in remaining flour and 2 to 4 tablespoons water (add 1 tablespoon at a time) to form dough.

Knead dough gently, and divide dough in half. Working with one portion at a time, pass dough through smooth rollers of pasta machine on widest setting. Generously dust dough with flour, and fold in half.

Repeat rolling, dusting, and folding procedure about 10 times or until dough is smooth and pliable.

Cut dough into 2 pieces. Pass each piece through rollers. Continue moving width gauge to narrower settings; pass dough through rollers once at each setting, dusting with flour, if needed.

Roll dough to thinness desired, about $1/16$ inch. Pass each dough sheet through the cutting rollers of machine.

Hang noodles over a wooden drying rack, or spread on a dry towel. Dry pasta no longer than 30 minutes. Repeat rolling and drying procedures with remaining portion of dough.

Combine boiling water, 1 teaspoon salt, and olive oil in a large Dutch oven. Add noodles; cook 2 to 3 minutes or until tender. Drain. Use in recipes that call for cooked noodles. **Yield: 10 cups.**

Homemade Pasta Techniques

To make Homemade Pasta, beat eggs in a large mixing bowl with a wire whisk.

Gradually add enough flour and water to form a soft dough.

Knead dough gently, and divide in half. Work with only one portion of dough at a time.

Pass one portion of dough through smooth rollers of pasta machine on widest setting. Repeat rolling, dusting, and folding procedure until dough is smooth and pliable.

Once smooth, pass dough through narrower settings until desired thinness is reached, dusting with flour, if needed.

Pass dough through desired cutting rollers of pasta machine.

Dry pasta over a wooden rack no longer than 30 minutes.

Cook Homemade Pasta 2 to 3 minutes or until tender. Serve the noodles plain or with a sauce.

Homemade Ravioli

1 cup ricotta cheese
1 (10-ounce) package frozen chopped spinach,
    thawed and squeezed almost dry
½ cup grated Parmesan cheese
2 egg yolks
2 tablespoons butter or margarine, softened
½ teaspoon ground nutmeg
½ teaspoon salt
¼ teaspoon pepper
1 recipe Homemade Pasta (recipe on page 10)
4 quarts boiling water
½ teaspoon salt
½ cup butter or margarine, melted
Grated Parmesan cheese
Chopped fresh parsley

Combine first 8 ingredients, stirring well; set aside.

Prepare dough for Homemade Pasta; divide dough into 4 equal portions. Set 2 portions aside. Pass each of 2 pieces of dough, one at a time, through rollers of pasta machine, starting at widest setting.

Continue moving width gauge to narrower settings, passing dough through rollers once at each setting and dusting with flour, if needed. Roll dough to desired thinness, about ¹⁄₁₆-inch thick, 6 inches wide, and 36 inches long.

Place 2 strips of dough on a lightly floured work surface. Roll each rectangle of dough with a ravioli rolling pin, using heavy pressure to make indentations. Spoon 1 teaspoon spinach mixture in center of each square of pattern on one rectangle of dough. Brush water along lines of pattern and edge of dough.

Align remaining rectangle over filled rectangle so rolled ravioli indentations are aligned. Use a fluted pastry wheel to cut through both layers of dough along pattern lines. Dry about 1 hour.

Repeat above rolling and filling procedures with remaining dough and filling ingredients.

Combine boiling water and ½ teaspoon salt in a large Dutch oven. Add half of ravioli; cook 10 to 12 minutes. Drain. Cook remaining ravioli.

Dip ravioli in melted butter; place on baking sheets in a single layer, and sprinkle with Parmesan cheese. Broil 6 inches from heat (with electric oven door partially opened) 3 to 4 minutes or until lightly browned. Place in serving container, and sprinkle with parsley. **Yield: 6 to 8 servings.**

Note: Homemade ravioli in no way resembles (nor should it) the canned versions. Although ravioli is often served with a mushroom or tomato sauce, a simple topping of melted butter and Parmesan cheese on this homemade version will win compliments every time.

Clockwise from top: Whole Wheat Linguine (page 13), Orange Noodles (page 13), Pimiento Pasta (page 14), and Broccoli Pasta (page 14)

Whole Wheat Linguine

1½ cups whole wheat flour
½ teaspoon salt
2 large eggs
2 tablespoons water
2 tablespoons olive oil
2 quarts water
¾ teaspoon salt
2 teaspoons vegetable oil

Position stainless steel chopping blade in food processor bowl. Combine first 5 ingredients in processor, and process until well blended.

Turn dough out onto a lightly floured surface, and knead 1 to 2 minutes. Shape dough into a ball, and place in a zip-top plastic bag. Chill dough 30 minutes.

Cut dough into 4 portions, and return 3 portions to bag. Pat remaining portion into a 4-inch square. Pass square through smooth rollers of pasta machine on widest setting. Fold dough crosswise into thirds. Repeat entire procedure with remaining 3 portions of dough.

Repeat rolling and folding about 10 times or until dough becomes smooth and pliable. Move rollers to next widest setting; pass dough through rollers.

Continue moving width gauge to narrower settings; pass dough through rollers once at each setting until 1/16-inch thickness, dusting lightly with flour, if needed.

Pass dough through linguine cutting rollers of machine. Hang pasta over a wooden rack, or spread on a dry towel for 30 minutes.

Combine water, ¾ teaspoon salt, and vegetable oil in a large Dutch oven; bring to a boil. Add pasta, and cook 1 to 2 minutes or until tender; drain. Serve with fresh tomato sauce or clam sauce. **Yield: about 4 servings.**

Orange Noodles

3 cups all-purpose flour
½ teaspoon salt
3 large eggs
¼ cup plus 1 tablespoon frozen orange juice
    concentrate, thawed and undiluted
2 tablespoons grated orange rind
3 quarts water
1 teaspoon salt
1 tablespoon vegetable oil

Position stainless steel chopping blade in food processor bowl. Combine first 5 ingredients in processor, and process until well blended.

Turn dough out onto a lightly floured surface, and knead 8 to 10 minutes. Shape dough into a ball, and place in a zip-top plastic bag. Chill dough 1 hour.

Cut dough into 8 portions, and return 7 portions to bag. Pat remaining portion into a 4-inch square. Pass square through smooth rollers of pasta machine on widest setting. Fold dough crosswise into thirds. Repeat entire procedure with remaining 7 portions of dough.

Repeat rolling and folding about 10 times or until dough becomes smooth and pliable. Move rollers to next widest setting; pass dough through rollers.

Continue moving width gauge to narrower settings; pass dough through rollers once at each setting until 1/16-inch thickness, dusting lightly with flour, if needed.

Pass dough through linguine cutting rollers of machine, or cut with fluted pastry cutter, if desired. Hang pasta over a wooden rack, or spread on a dry towel for 30 minutes.

Combine water, 1 teaspoon salt, and oil in a large Dutch oven; bring to a boil. Add pasta, and cook 1 to 2 minutes or until tender; drain. Serve immediately, plain or buttered. **Yield: 6 servings.**

Pimiento Pasta

2 (4-ounce) jars sliced pimiento, drained
1 large egg
1 tablespoon dry white wine
3 to 3½ cups all-purpose flour
½ teaspoon salt
3 quarts water
1½ teaspoons salt
1 tablespoon olive oil or vegetable oil

Position stainless steel chopping blade in food processor bowl. Combine first 5 ingredients in processor, and process until well blended.

Turn dough out onto a lightly floured surface; knead until smooth. Shape dough into a ball, and place in a zip-top plastic bag. Chill dough 1 hour.

Cut dough into 8 portions, and return 7 portions to bag. Pat remaining portion into a 4-inch square. Pass square through smooth rollers of pasta machine on widest setting. Fold dough crosswise into thirds. Repeat entire procedure with remaining 7 portions of dough.

Repeat rolling and folding about 10 times or until dough becomes smooth and pliable. Move rollers to next widest setting; pass dough through rollers.

Continue moving width gauge to narrower settings; pass dough through rollers once at each setting until ¹⁄₁₆-inch thickness, dusting lightly with flour, if needed.

Pass dough through desired cutting rollers of machine. Hang pasta over a wooden rack, shape into nests, or spread on a dry towel for 30 minutes.

Combine water, 1½ teaspoons salt, and oil in a large Dutch oven; bring to a boil. Add pasta, and cook 1 to 2 minutes or until tender; drain. Serve immediately, plain, buttered, or with a chicken or meat sauce. **Yield: 6 servings.**

Broccoli Pasta

1 (10-ounce) package frozen chopped broccoli
4 cups all-purpose flour
3 large eggs
1 tablespoon lemon juice
1 teaspoon salt
3 quarts water
1½ teaspoons salt
1 tablespoon olive oil or vegetable oil

Cook broccoli according to package directions; drain. Place on paper towels; pat dry.

Position stainless steel chopping blade in food processor bowl. Add broccoli and next 4 ingredients. Process until well blended.

Turn dough out onto a lightly floured surface, and knead about 5 minutes. Shape dough into a ball, and place in a zip-top plastic bag. Chill dough at least 1 hour.

Cut dough into 8 portions, and return 7 portions to bag. Pat remaining portion into a 4-inch square. Pass square through smooth rollers of pasta machine on widest setting. Fold dough crosswise into thirds. Repeat entire procedure with remaining 7 portions of dough.

Repeat rolling and folding 10 times or until dough becomes smooth and pliable. Move rollers to next widest setting; pass dough through rollers.

Continue moving width gauge to narrower settings; pass dough through rollers once at each setting until ¹⁄₁₆-inch thickness, dusting lightly with flour, if needed.

Pass dough through desired cutting rollers of machine. Hang pasta over a wooden rack, or spread on a dry towel for 30 minutes.

Combine 3 quarts water, 1½ teaspoons salt, and oil in a large Dutch oven; bring to a boil. Add pasta, and cook 3 to 4 minutes or until tender. Drain; serve immediately, plain or topped with Parmesan cheese or a sauce. **Yield: 6 servings.**

Note: Substitute 1 (10-ounce) package frozen spinach for broccoli, if desired.

Mainstay Meats

Move over spaghetti and lasagna—manicotti, fettuccine, and tortellini now have equal space in the pantry. Turn these shapes into main dishes to add spark to weeknight or weekend dining.

Pot Roast in Sour Cream, Roquefort Beef Roulades, Veal Marsala

Party Pasta with Prosciutto, Fettuccine with Ham and Peas, Tortellini au Gratin

Red Pepper Round Steak, Classic Beef Stroganoff, One-Step Lasagna, Cavatini

Italian Zucchini Spaghetti, Beefy Tomato-Stuffed Shells, Pasticcio

Meaty Spaghetti with Mushrooms (page 24)

Pot Roast in Sour Cream

1 (3½- to 4-pound) boneless rump roast
2 tablespoons vegetable oil
½ cup water
½ teaspoon beef-flavored bouillon granules
1 bay leaf
½ teaspoon salt
½ teaspoon coarsely ground pepper
2 onions, quartered
2 carrots, scraped and cut into pieces
2 tablespoons all-purpose flour
3 tablespoons water
1 (8-ounce) carton sour cream
Hot cooked noodles

Brown roast on all sides in hot oil in a large Dutch oven. Combine ½ cup water and bouillon granules; add to Dutch oven. Add bay leaf, salt, and pepper.

Cover, reduce heat, and simmer 2½ hours. Add onion and carrot; cover and cook 30 minutes or until vegetables and meat are tender.

Remove roast and vegetables from Dutch oven; keep warm. Remove and discard bay leaf. Combine flour and 3 tablespoons water; stir into pan drippings. Cook, stirring constantly, until gravy is smooth and thickened.

Add sour cream and vegetables to gravy, and cook, stirring constantly, until vegetables are thoroughly heated. Place cooked noodles on a serving platter. Slice roast, and arrange over noodles. Serve with gravy. **Yield: 6 to 8 servings.**

Roquefort Beef Roulades

1 (3-ounce) can sliced mushrooms, undrained
2 (1-pound) round steaks
¼ teaspoon pepper
½ cup chopped onion, divided
1 (4-ounce) package Roquefort cheese, divided
2 tablespoons all-purpose flour
2 tablespoons vegetable oil
1 (12-ounce) can vegetable juice
2 tablespoons Worcestershire sauce
Hot cooked noodles

Drain mushrooms, reserving liquid; set aside.

Trim excess fat from steak. Cut each steak into 3 pieces, and pound to ¼-inch thickness, using a smooth-surfaced meat mallet.

Sprinkle pepper, mushrooms, half of onion, and half of cheese on steaks; roll up, and secure with wooden picks. Dredge steaks in flour, coating evenly. Brown steaks in hot oil in a large skillet; drain.

Return steaks to skillet, and add vegetable juice, reserved mushroom liquid, Worcestershire sauce, and remaining onion. Bring to a boil; cover, reduce heat, and simmer 45 minutes.

Arrange steaks on a platter over hot cooked noodles. Add remaining cheese to sauce, stirring until blended. Spoon sauce over steaks. **Yield: 6 servings.**

Keep the Pasta Platter Hot

Pasta is best served piping hot, but it cools quickly when placed on serving dishes that are at room temperature. To avoid the cool down, preheat the serving platter or bowls. Warm heat-proof dishes in a 250° oven about 10 minutes, or drain some of the hot pasta cooking liquid into the serving bowl and let stand about 2 minutes. Pour off the water, and transfer the pasta to the dish.

Red Pepper Round Steak

Red Pepper Round Steak

1 **(1-pound) round steak**
½ **teaspoon salt**
⅛ **teaspoon pepper**
2 **tablespoons chopped onion**
2 **tablespoons vegetable oil**
1 **large sweet red pepper, chopped**
1 **beef-flavored bouillon cube**
1 **cup hot water**
1 **(14½-ounce) can tomato wedges, drained**
1 **tablespoon cornstarch**
¼ **cup water**
2 **teaspoons soy sauce**
Hot cooked noodles

Partially freeze steak; slice diagonally across grain into ¼-inch-wide strips. Cut strips into 2-inch pieces. Sprinkle steak with salt and pepper.

Cook steak and onion in hot oil in a heavy skillet, stirring constantly, until steak is browned. Add chopped red pepper.

Dissolve bouillon cube in 1 cup hot water; add to steak, and bring to a boil. Cover, reduce heat, and simmer 40 minutes. Add tomatoes.

Combine cornstarch, ¼ cup water, and soy sauce, stirring well; stir into steak mixture. Bring to a boil, and cook, stirring constantly, 1 minute. Serve over noodles. **Yield: 4 servings.**

Classic Beef Stroganoff

1 pound (½-inch-thick) boneless sirloin steak
½ pound sliced fresh mushrooms
¼ cup chopped onion
1 clove garlic, crushed
3 tablespoons butter or margarine, melted
2 tablespoons all-purpose flour
1 (10½-ounce) can beef consommé
3 tablespoons dry sherry
1 tablespoon lemon juice
¼ teaspoon pepper
1 (8-ounce) carton sour cream
Parslied Noodles
Garnish: fresh parsley sprigs

Partially freeze steak; slice steak diagonally across grain into 3- x ¼-inch strips; set aside.

Cook mushrooms, onion, and garlic in butter in a large skillet, stirring constantly, until vegetables are tender.

Add steak; cook over medium-high heat until browned, stirring frequently. Add flour and next 4 ingredients, stirring well. Bring to a boil; reduce heat, and simmer 15 minutes, stirring occasionally.

Stir in sour cream; cook until thoroughly heated (do not boil). Serve over Parslied Noodles. Garnish, if desired. **Yield: 4 servings.**

Parslied Noodles

4 ounces medium egg noodles, uncooked
2 tablespoons butter or margarine, melted
2 teaspoons chopped fresh parsley

Cook noodles according to package directions; drain well. Combine noodles, butter, and parsley in a large bowl; toss gently. Serve immediately. **Yield: 3 cups.**

Classic Beef Stroganoff Techniques

Stir consommé into meat mixture. Beef consommé is a clarified beef broth used frequently as a flavorful sauce base.

Do not boil mixture after adding sour cream; intense heat causes sour cream to curdle.

Gently toss hot cooked noodles with melted butter and chopped fresh parsley. Top with stroganoff, and serve immediately.

Classic Beef Stroganoff

Cream Cheese Lasagna

Cream Cheese Lasagna

1 pound ground beef
½ cup chopped onion
1 (8-ounce) can tomato sauce
1 (6-ounce) can tomato paste
¼ cup water
1 tablespoon dried parsley flakes
2 teaspoons dried Italian seasoning
1 teaspoon beef-flavored bouillon granules
¼ teaspoon garlic powder
1 (8-ounce) package cream cheese, softened
1 cup cottage cheese
¼ cup sour cream
2 large eggs, beaten
1 (8-ounce) package lasagna noodles, cooked
    and drained
1 (3½-ounce) package sliced pepperoni
2 cups (8 ounces) shredded mozzarella cheese
½ cup grated Parmesan cheese
Garnish: green pepper rings

Cook beef and onion in a heavy skillet, stirring until meat browns and crumbles; drain. Return to skillet, and stir in tomato sauce and next 6 ingredients; cook over low heat 10 minutes.

Combine cream cheese, cottage cheese, sour cream, and eggs; stir well.

Spoon a small amount of meat sauce into a lightly greased 13- x 9- x 2-inch baking dish. Layer with half each of lasagna noodles, cheese mixture, pepperoni, meat sauce, and mozzarella cheese.

Repeat layers; sprinkle with Parmesan cheese.

Cover and bake at 350° for 30 minutes. Let stand 10 minutes before serving. Garnish, if desired. **Yield: 6 servings.**

Microwave Directions:

Crumble ground beef into a 2-quart baking dish; add onion. Cover with wax paper, and microwave at HIGH 4 to 6 minutes or until meat is no longer pink, stirring twice. Drain.

Stir in tomato sauce and next 6 ingredients.

Cover and microwave at HIGH 2 to 3 minutes or until thoroughly heated, stirring once.

Combine cream cheese, cottage cheese, sour cream, and eggs; stir well.

Layer ingredients in a lightly greased 13- x 9- x 2-inch baking dish as directed.

Cover and microwave at MEDIUM HIGH (70% power) 6 to 8 minutes, giving dish a half-turn after 5 minutes. Let stand 10 minutes before serving. Garnish, if desired.

One-Step Lasagna

1 pound lean ground beef
1 (15¼-ounce) jar spaghetti sauce
½ cup water
¼ cup dry red wine
8 lasagna noodles, uncooked
2 cups cottage cheese
3 cups (12 ounces) shredded mozzarella cheese
½ cup grated Parmesan cheese

Crumble beef into a microwave-safe colander; place colander in a 9-inch pieplate. Cover and microwave at HIGH 5 to 6 minutes or until meat is no longer pink, stirring after 3 minutes.

Combine beef, spaghetti sauce, water, and wine. Spread one-third of meat sauce in a lightly greased 13- x 9- x 2-inch baking dish.

Arrange 4 uncooked lasagna noodles on sauce. Layer 1 cup cottage cheese and 1 cup mozzarella cheese over noodles. Spoon half of remaining sauce over cheese.

Repeat layers; sprinkle with Parmesan cheese. Cover tightly with heavy-duty plastic wrap; fold back a small corner of wrap.

Microwave at MEDIUM (50% power) 32 to 35 minutes, giving dish a half-turn after 15 minutes. Sprinkle with remaining 1 cup mozzarella cheese, and microwave, uncovered, at MEDIUM 2 minutes. Let stand 10 minutes. **Yield: 6 servings.**

Specialty Lasagna

Specialty Lasagna

1½ pounds ground beef
¾ cup chopped onion
3 cloves garlic, minced
2 (8-ounce) cans tomato sauce
1 (6-ounce) can tomato paste
1 (4-ounce) can sliced mushrooms, drained
¼ cup red wine vinegar
2 teaspoons dried Italian seasoning
½ teaspoon dried oregano
¼ teaspoon garlic powder
¼ teaspoon salt
¼ teaspoon pepper
1 (8-ounce) package cream cheese, softened
¾ cup ricotta cheese
½ cup sour cream
1 large egg
6 lasagna noodles, uncooked
1¼ cups (5 ounces) shredded mozzarella
    cheese
½ cup grated Parmesan cheese
1 (6-ounce) package mozzarella cheese slices,
    cut into ½-inch-wide strips

Crumble ground beef into a 2-quart baking dish; add onion and minced garlic. Cover with wax paper; microwave at HIGH 5 to 6 minutes or until meat is no longer pink, stirring twice. Drain well.

Stir in tomato sauce and next 8 ingredients. Cover and microwave at HIGH 3 to 4 minutes or until thoroughly heated, stirring once.

Beat cream cheese until smooth. Stir in ricotta cheese, sour cream, and egg.

Place noodles in a 13- x 9- x 2-inch baking dish; add water to cover. Cover tightly with heavy-duty plastic wrap; fold back a small corner of wrap to allow steam to escape. Microwave at HIGH 12 to 13 minutes, rearranging noodles after 7 minutes. Drain; pat dry.

Layer half each of cooked noodles, cream cheese mixture, and meat mixture in a greased 13- x 9- x 2-inch baking dish. Sprinkle meat mixture with shredded mozzarella cheese. Repeat layers. Sprinkle with Parmesan cheese.

Cover and microwave at MEDIUM HIGH (70% power) 10 to 12 minutes or until thoroughly heated, giving dish a half-turn after 7 minutes.

Arrange mozzarella strips in a lattice design over lasagna. Cover lasagna, and microwave at MEDIUM HIGH 2 to 3 minutes or until cheese melts. Let stand 5 minutes. **Yield: 6 servings.**

Specialty Lasagna Techniques

Cook lasagna noodles covered in water. Use tongs to carefully rearrange noodles halfway through cooking time.

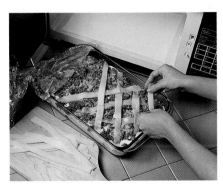

For a decorative topping, add strips of mozzarella cheese in a lattice design during last 3 minutes of cooking.

Meaty Spaghetti with Mushrooms

(pictured on page 15)

½ pound ground beef
½ pound hot Italian sausage
1 medium onion, chopped
¾ pound fresh mushrooms, sliced
1 cup diced green pepper
4 cloves garlic, minced
3 tablespoons olive oil
2 (16-ounce) cans whole tomatoes, undrained
    and coarsely chopped
2 (8-ounce) cans tomato sauce
2 (6-ounce) cans tomato paste
¾ cup water
½ cup dry white wine
1 to 2 tablespoons sugar
1½ teaspoons dried basil
1½ teaspoons dried oregano
1 bay leaf
½ teaspoon salt
½ teaspoon garlic powder
¼ teaspoon ground thyme
¼ teaspoon freshly ground pepper
1 (12-ounce) package thin spaghetti, uncooked
Freshly grated Parmesan cheese

Cook first 3 ingredients in a large Dutch oven, stirring until meat browns and crumbles. Drain well, and set aside.

Cook mushrooms, green pepper, and garlic in olive oil in Dutch oven until tender; add meat mixture. Add tomatoes and next 12 ingredients. Bring to a boil.

Cover, reduce heat, and simmer 25 minutes, stirring occasionally. Uncover and cook 20 minutes, stirring occasionally.

Cook spaghetti according to package directions; drain.

Remove bay leaf from spaghetti sauce. Serve sauce over hot cooked spaghetti; sprinkle with Parmesan cheese. **Yield: 8 servings.**

Quick Spaghetti

1 large onion, chopped
1 green pepper, chopped
1 pound ground beef
1 (3-ounce) package sliced pepperoni,
    chopped
1 (32-ounce) jar spaghetti sauce with
    mushrooms
1 (12-ounce) package spaghetti, uncooked
1 cup (4 ounces) shredded mozzarella cheese
1 tablespoon grated Parmesan cheese

Cook first 4 ingredients in a large skillet over medium heat, stirring until beef browns and crumbles. Remove from heat; drain. Return mixture to skillet.

Add spaghetti sauce to beef mixture, and bring to a boil. Cover, reduce heat, and simmer 20 minutes, stirring occasionally.

Cook spaghetti according to package directions, omitting salt. Drain. Arrange on an ovenproof platter; spoon meat sauce on top. Sprinkle mozzarella cheese over sauce.

Bake at 400° for 3 to 5 minutes. Remove from oven; top with Parmesan cheese. Serve immediately. **Yield: 6 servings.**

Quick Spaghetti

Casserole Spaghetti

1½ pounds ground chuck
1 green pepper, chopped
1 large onion, chopped
½ cup chopped celery
2 cloves garlic, crushed
1 (10¾-ounce) can cream of mushroom soup, undiluted
¾ cup water
1 (16-ounce) can tomatoes, undrained and chopped
2 tablespoons chili powder
½ teaspoon salt
¼ teaspoon pepper
1 (8-ounce) package spaghetti, uncooked
2 ounces sharp Cheddar cheese, cut into ½-inch cubes
1 (5-ounce) jar pimiento-stuffed olives, drained
¾ cup (3 ounces) shredded sharp Cheddar cheese

Cook first 5 ingredients in a Dutch oven, stirring until meat browns and crumbles; drain and return to Dutch oven.

Stir in soup and next 5 ingredients.

Bring soup mixture to a boil over medium heat. Cover, reduce heat, and simmer 1 hour, stirring occasionally.

Cook spaghetti according to package directions; drain.

Stir spaghetti, cheese cubes, and olives into meat sauce. Spoon into a lightly greased 11- x 7- x 1½-inch baking dish.

Cover and bake at 325° for 20 minutes or until thoroughly heated. Sprinkle with ¾ cup shredded cheese, and bake, uncovered, 10 additional minutes. **Yield: 6 to 8 servings.**

Cavatini

1 (16-ounce) package shell macaroni, uncooked
1 pound ground beef
1 pound mild ground pork sausage
1 medium onion, chopped
1 green pepper, chopped
1 (3½-ounce) package sliced pepperoni, chopped
1 (28-ounce) can crushed tomatoes, undrained
1 (26½-ounce) can spaghetti sauce
1 (16-ounce) jar mild salsa
1 (4-ounce) can sliced mushrooms, drained
1 (10-ounce) jar pepperoncini salad peppers, drained and sliced
1 cup grated Parmesan cheese
4 cups (16 ounces) shredded mozzarella cheese

Cook macaroni according to package directions; drain and set aside.

Cook ground beef and next 3 ingredients in a large skillet over medium heat, stirring until meat browns and crumbles. Drain well; set aside.

Combine chopped pepperoni and next 5 ingredients in a large bowl; stir in meat mixture and pasta shells.

Spoon half of pasta mixture into 2 lightly greased 11- x 7- x 1½-inch baking dishes; sprinkle each casserole with ¼ cup Parmesan and 1 cup mozzarella cheeses. Top with remaining pasta mixture.

Bake at 350° for 30 minutes or until heated; top with remaining cheeses. Bake 5 additional minutes. **Yield: 6 servings per casserole.**

Note: Unbaked casseroles may be frozen up to 3 months (freeze cheeses for topping separately). Thaw casseroles in refrigerator 24 hours; let stand at room temperature 30 minutes. Bake at 350° for 40 minutes; sprinkle with cheeses. Bake 5 additional minutes.

Pasticcio

1½ pounds ground beef
1 cup chopped onion
1 (16-ounce) can tomatoes, undrained and
     chopped
1 (6-ounce) can tomato paste
¼ teaspoon dried thyme
1¾ teaspoons salt, divided
1 (8-ounce) package elbow macaroni,
     uncooked
½ cup crumbled feta cheese
4 egg whites, lightly beaten
½ cup butter or margarine
½ cup all-purpose flour
¼ teaspoon ground cinnamon
1 quart milk
4 egg yolks, lightly beaten

Cook ground beef and onion in a large skillet over medium heat, stirring until beef browns and crumbles; drain.

Stir in tomatoes, tomato paste, thyme, and ¾ teaspoon salt; bring to a boil. Cover, reduce heat, and simmer 30 minutes, stirring often.

Cook macaroni according to package directions, adding ¼ teaspoon salt; drain. Stir in feta cheese and egg whites. Add to beef mixture; stir well. Spoon mixture into a lightly greased 13- x 9- x 2-inch baking dish.

Melt butter in a heavy saucepan over low heat; add flour and cinnamon, stirring until smooth. Cook, stirring constantly, 1 minute. Gradually add milk; cook over medium heat, stirring constantly, until mixture is thickened and bubbly. Stir in remaining ¾ teaspoon salt. Gradually stir about one-fourth of hot mixture into yolks; add to remaining hot mixture, stirring constantly. Cook, stirring constantly, 1 minute.

Pour sauce over beef mixture; bake at 350° for 35 to 40 minutes. Remove from oven; let stand 10 minutes. **Yield: 8 servings.**

Pizza Casserole

1 pound lean ground beef
1 large onion, chopped
1 green pepper, chopped
½ teaspoon garlic salt
¼ teaspoon pepper
¼ teaspoon dried oregano
¼ teaspoon dried basil
1 (14-ounce) jar pizza sauce
1 (8-ounce) package macaroni, uncooked
1 (3½-ounce) package sliced pepperoni
1 (4-ounce) package shredded mozzarella
     cheese

Cook ground beef, onion, and green pepper in a large Dutch oven, stirring until meat browns and crumbles. Drain well.

Add garlic salt and next 4 ingredients. Stir well; cover, reduce heat, and simmer 15 minutes.

Cook macaroni according to package directions, omitting salt; drain. Add to meat mixture; stir well. Spoon into a lightly greased 13- x 9- x 2-inch baking dish; top evenly with pepperoni.

Cover and bake at 350° for 20 minutes; top with cheese, and bake, uncovered, 5 additional minutes. **Yield: 6 to 8 servings.**

Did You Know?

Pasticcio, a term derived from the French "pastiche," literally means hodgepodge or potpourri. That's the perfect description for this casserole featuring elbow macaroni layered with a tomato-meat sauce. Feta cheese and cinnamon add authenticity to this Greek dish.

Beefy Tomato-Stuffed Shells

24 jumbo pasta shells, uncooked
1 pound ground beef
½ cup minced onion
½ teaspoon pepper
¼ teaspoon garlic powder
¼ teaspoon dried crushed red pepper
1¼ cups beef broth
1 (7-ounce) jar sun-dried tomatoes in oil,
    drained
¼ cup pine nuts, toasted
¼ cup fresh basil leaves
2 tablespoons chopped fresh parsley
2 cloves garlic, sliced
¼ cup olive oil
⅓ cup grated Parmesan cheese
1 (32-ounce) jar spaghetti sauce
1½ cups (6 ounces) shredded mozzarella
    cheese
1 to 2 tablespoons chopped fresh parsley

Cook shells according to package directions;
drain and set aside.

Cook ground beef and onion in a large skillet,
stirring until meat browns and crumbles; drain.
Add pepper, garlic powder, and red pepper. Cover
and set aside.

Combine beef broth and next 5 ingredients in
container of an electric blender; cover and process
until well blended. Add olive oil in a slow, steady
stream, and process until combined.

Stir tomato mixture into ground beef mixture.
Stir in Parmesan cheese.

Spoon 1 heaping tablespoonful of ground beef
mixture into each shell. Arrange shells in a lightly
greased 13- x 9- x 2-inch baking dish or ovenproof serving dish. Pour spaghetti sauce over top.

Cover and bake at 375° for 20 to 30 minutes
or until thoroughly heated. Uncover; sprinkle
with mozzarella cheese, and bake 5 additional
minutes or until cheese melts. Sprinkle with
chopped parsley. **Yield: 6 servings.**

Beefy Tomato-Stuffed Shells Techniques

Pine nuts, or pignoli, taste slightly like almonds
but are much smaller and have no skins. Process
with beef broth and other ingredients in a blender
or food processor.

Cook pasta shells in advance so that they will
have cooled before being filled with ground beef
mixture.

Beefy Tomato-Stuffed Shells

Saucy Manicotti

Saucy Manicotti

¾ pound ground chuck
¾ pound ground hot pork sausage
1 large onion, chopped
5 cloves garlic, minced
2 (15-ounce) cans tomato sauce
1 (14½-ounce) can tomatoes, undrained and
    chopped
1 (6-ounce) can tomato paste
1½ teaspoons dried oregano
1½ teaspoons dried basil
1 teaspoon sugar
¼ teaspoon salt
¼ teaspoon pepper
1 (8-ounce) package manicotti shells,
    uncooked
1 (8-ounce) package cream cheese, softened
½ (8-ounce) carton cream cheese with chives
    and onions
4 cups (16 ounces) shredded mozzarella cheese
1 (16-ounce) carton ricotta cheese
¾ cup grated Parmesan cheese
4 cloves garlic, crushed
¾ teaspoon pepper
½ teaspoon dried oregano

Cook first 4 ingredients in a large Dutch oven over medium heat, stirring until meat browns and crumbles; drain well. Add tomato sauce and next 7 ingredients; bring to a boil. Cover, reduce heat, and simmer 2½ hours, stirring occasionally.

Cook manicotti shells according to package directions; drain and let cool to touch.

Beat cream cheeses in a large bowl at medium speed of an electric mixer until smooth. Add mozzarella cheese and remaining 5 ingredients; stir well. Stuff mixture evenly into cooked shells.

Spoon half of sauce evenly into 2 greased 2½-quart shallow baking dishes. Arrange stuffed shells over sauce. Spoon remaining sauce over shells.

Bake at 350° for 30 to 40 minutes. Let stand 5 minutes before serving. **Yield: 8 servings.**

Cannelloni

3 cups tomato sauce
2 tablespoons grated Parmesan cheese
¼ cup diced onion
1 teaspoon minced garlic
2 tablespoons olive oil
1 (10-ounce) package frozen chopped spinach,
    thawed and drained
1 pound ground beef
2 large eggs, lightly beaten
⅓ cup grated Parmesan cheese
2 tablespoons whipping cream
½ teaspoon dried oregano
12 cannelloni shells, cooked
⅓ cup butter or margarine
⅓ cup all-purpose flour
1 cup milk
1 cup whipping cream
⅛ teaspoon ground white pepper
2 tablespoons butter or margarine

Combine tomato sauce and 2 tablespoons Parmesan cheese in a saucepan; cook over medium heat, stirring constantly, until heated. Spread 1 cup tomato mixture in a lightly greased 13- x 9- x 2-inch baking dish; set aside remaining sauce.

Cook onion and garlic in olive oil in a large skillet until tender. Add spinach, and cook until just tender. Remove from skillet, and set aside.

Brown beef in skillet over medium heat, stirring until it crumbles; drain. Stir in spinach mixture, eggs, and next 3 ingredients.

Stuff cannelloni shells with meat mixture and place on tomato mixture in baking dish; set aside.

Melt ⅓ cup butter in a heavy saucepan over low heat; add flour, stirring until smooth. Cook, stirring constantly, 1 minute. Add milk and 1 cup whipping cream; cook over medium heat, stirring constantly, until thickened. Stir in pepper. Pour sauce over cannelloni; top with reserved tomato mixture. Dot with 2 tablespoons butter. Bake, uncovered, at 375° for 20 minutes. **Yield: 6 servings.**

Stuffed Veal Cutlets

6 (4-ounce) veal cutlets
6 slices prosciutto (about 5 ounces)
4 ounces fontina cheese, cut into 5 strips
¼ teaspoon salt
¼ teaspoon pepper
½ cup all-purpose flour
1 tablespoon butter or margarine, melted
1 tablespoon vegetable oil
1 cup dry white wine
Hot cooked spaghetti

Place cutlets between sheets of heavy-duty plastic wrap; flatten to ⅛-inch thickness, using a meat mallet or rolling pin. Wrap a prosciutto slice around each cheese strip, and place in center of each cutlet. Fold ends of veal cutlets over prosciutto and cheese; fold sides over, and secure with a wooden pick.

Sprinkle cutlets with salt and pepper; dredge in flour. Brown on all sides in butter and oil in a heavy skillet. Remove and keep warm.

Add wine to skillet; boil until wine is reduced by half. Add veal; cover and simmer 5 minutes. Serve over spaghetti. **Yield: 6 servings.**

Veal Marsala

¾ cup all-purpose flour
½ teaspoon salt
⅛ teaspoon freshly ground pepper
1¼ pounds thin veal cutlets
½ cup butter or margarine, melted
1¼ cups Marsala wine
Hot cooked vermicelli

Combine flour, salt, and pepper. Dredge veal in flour mixture, and cook in butter 1 to 2 minutes on each side. Place veal on a serving platter; keep warm.

Add wine to skillet, scraping bottom of skillet to loosen browned particles. Cook until bubbly; pour over veal. Serve over vermicelli. **Yield: 4 to 6 servings.**

Note: You may substitute 1 cup dry white wine plus ¼ cup brandy for Marsala wine.

Pork Piccata

2 (¾-pound) pork tenderloins
½ cup all-purpose flour
½ teaspoon salt
¼ teaspoon pepper
3 tablespoons olive oil
½ cup dry white wine
½ cup lemon juice
3 tablespoons butter or margarine
¼ cup chopped fresh parsley
1½ tablespoons capers
Hot cooked fettuccine
Garnishes: lemon slices, fresh parsley sprigs

Cut each tenderloin into 6 (2-ounce) medaillons. Place medaillons, cut side down, between 2 sheets of heavy-duty plastic wrap; flatten to ¼-inch thickness, using a meat mallet or rolling pin.

Combine flour, salt, and pepper; dredge pork in flour mixture.

Cook half of pork in 1½ tablespoons olive oil in a large skillet over medium heat about 2 minutes on each side or until lightly browned. Remove from skillet; keep warm. Repeat procedure.

Add wine and lemon juice to skillet; cook until thoroughly heated. Add butter, chopped parsley, and capers, stirring until butter melts.

Arrange pork over pasta; drizzle with wine mixture. Garnish, if desired. Serve immediately. **Yield: 6 servings.**

Pork Marsala

1 (1-pound) pork tenderloin
1 tablespoon butter or margarine
1 tablespoon vegetable oil
1 clove garlic, minced
½ cup Marsala wine
½ cup dry red wine
1 tablespoon tomato paste
½ pound fresh mushroom caps
1 tablespoon chopped fresh parsley
Hot cooked noodles

Cut tenderloin into 4 equal pieces. Place each piece between two sheets of heavy-duty plastic wrap; flatten to ¼-inch thickness, using a meat mallet or rolling pin.

Heat butter and oil in a large, heavy skillet over medium heat. Add pork, and cook 3 to 4 minutes on each side or until browned. Remove pork from skillet, and keep warm.

Cook garlic in pan drippings in skillet; add wines and tomato paste, stirring until blended. Add mushroom caps, and simmer 3 to 5 minutes. Return pork to skillet, and cook until thoroughly heated. Sprinkle with parsley; serve over noodles. **Yield: 4 servings.**

Pasta Cooking Technique

Add pasta to boiling water in small batches. A few drops of oil added to the water prevents pasta from sticking together.

Ham and Swiss on Noodles

16 ounces egg noodles, uncooked
¼ cup sliced green onions
½ cup butter or margarine, divided
1 (4-ounce) can sliced mushrooms, drained
1 (10-ounce) package frozen English peas, thawed and drained
¼ cup all-purpose flour
3 cups milk
½ teaspoon salt
½ teaspoon ground white pepper
2 cups (8 ounces) shredded Swiss cheese
2 cups cubed cooked ham
1 cup chopped canned tomatoes, drained

Cook noodles according to package directions. Drain and keep noodles warm.

Cook green onions in 2 tablespoons melted butter in a large heavy saucepan 3 minutes; add mushrooms and peas, and cook until heated. Remove from saucepan, and set aside.

Melt remaining 6 tablespoons butter in saucepan; add flour, stirring until smooth. Cook, stirring constantly, 1 minute. Gradually add milk, and cook over medium heat, stirring constantly, until mixture is thickened and bubbly. Add salt and pepper, stirring well. Add cheese, and stir until mixture is smooth.

Add vegetables, ham, and tomatoes; mix well. Cook until thoroughly heated. Serve over noodles. **Yield: 8 servings.**

Spaghetti-Ham Pie

6 ounces spaghetti, uncooked
4 cloves garlic, minced
2½ tablespoons olive oil
¼ cup all-purpose flour
¼ teaspoon salt
⅛ teaspoon freshly ground pepper
¾ cup half-and-half
1½ cups milk
¼ to ½ cup chopped cooked ham
¼ cup grated Parmesan cheese, divided

Cook spaghetti according to package directions; drain and set aside.

Cook garlic in olive oil in a Dutch oven over medium heat, stirring constantly, 5 minutes. Stir in flour, salt, and pepper. Cook, stirring constantly, 1 minute.

Add half-and-half and milk; cook over medium heat, stirring constantly, until thickened and bubbly. Stir in spaghetti.

Spoon half of spaghetti mixture into a lightly greased 9-inch pieplate; sprinkle with ham and 2 tablespoons Parmesan cheese. Top with remaining spaghetti mixture; sprinkle with remaining 2 tablespoons Parmesan cheese.

Bake at 425° for 15 to 20 minutes or until lightly browned. **Yield: 6 servings.**

Fettuccine with Ham and Peas

2 cloves garlic, crushed
1 tablespoon butter or margarine, melted
½ pound thinly sliced cooked ham
1 cup frozen English peas, thawed
12 ounces fettuccine, uncooked
½ cup butter or margarine, softened
1 cup grated Parmesan cheese
1 (8-ounce) carton sour cream
½ teaspoon pepper

Cook garlic in 1 tablespoon melted butter in a large skillet over medium heat. Stir in ham and peas; cook, stirring constantly, 3 to 5 minutes. Remove from heat; cover and keep warm.

Cook fettuccine according to package directions, omitting salt. Drain well; place in a large serving bowl. Add ½ cup softened butter, stirring until completely melted; add Parmesan cheese and sour cream, stirring gently to coat well.

Fold ham mixture into fettuccine mixture. Add pepper; toss gently. Serve immediately. **Yield: 6 servings.**

Fettuccine with Ham and Peas Techniques

Stack several slices of ham on cutting board; cut ham into ¼-inch slices. Repeat procedure with remaining ham slices.

Thaw peas in microwave oven at HIGH 1 to 2 minutes, stirring to melt ice crystals.

Fettuccine with Ham and Peas

Deluxe Macaroni and Cheese

Deluxe Macaroni and Cheese

1 (8-ounce) package elbow macaroni,
    uncooked
2 cups (8 ounces) shredded Cheddar cheese
2 cups cottage cheese
1 (8-ounce) carton sour cream
1 cup diced cooked ham
3 tablespoons finely chopped onion
1 large egg, lightly beaten
¼ teaspoon salt
¼ teaspoon pepper
1 cup soft breadcrumbs
2 tablespoons butter or margarine, melted
¼ teaspoon paprika
Garnishes: sliced cherry tomatoes, fresh
    parsley sprigs

Cook macaroni according to package directions; drain well.

Place macaroni and next 8 ingredients in a large bowl; stir gently to combine. Spoon mixture into a lightly greased 2-quart baking dish.

Combine breadcrumbs, melted butter, and paprika in a small bowl, stirring well. Sprinkle breadcrumb mixture diagonally across top of casserole, forming stripes.

Bake at 350° for 30 to 40 minutes or until golden. Garnish, if desired. **Yield: 6 servings.**

Chorizo Carbonara

1 (16-ounce) package spaghetti, uncooked
½ pound chorizo sausage, crumbled
1 cup half-and-half
2 cups (8 ounces) shredded Monterey Jack
    cheese with peppers
1 (4½-ounce) can chopped green chiles,
    drained
½ teaspoon ground cumin

Cook spaghetti according to package directions; drain and set aside.

Brown sausage in a nonstick skillet over medium heat. Drain sausage well on paper towels, and set aside.

Heat half-and-half in a small saucepan.

Combine half-and-half, sausage, spaghetti, cheese, and remaining ingredients in a large bowl, tossing until cheese melts. Serve immediately. **Yield: 8 servings.**

Italian Zucchini Spaghetti

1½ pounds hot Italian sausage links, cut into
    bite-size pieces
2 medium-size green peppers, seeded and
    chopped
1 cup chopped onion
2 cloves garlic, minced
3 medium zucchini, coarsely shredded
2 cups chopped peeled tomato
1 (7½-ounce) can tomatoes and jalapeño
    peppers, undrained
1 teaspoon dried Italian seasoning
1 teaspoon chili powder
½ teaspoon salt
1 teaspoon lemon juice
½ teaspoon hot sauce
½ cup grated Parmesan cheese
Hot cooked spaghetti

Cook first 4 ingredients in a Dutch oven, stirring until meat browns; drain well.

Add zucchini and next 7 ingredients; cook over medium heat 10 to 15 minutes or until zucchini is tender, stirring occasionally. Remove from heat; stir in cheese. Serve sauce over spaghetti. **Yield: 8 servings.**

Lasagna Pizza

16 lasagna noodles, uncooked
4 cups (16 ounces) shredded mozzarella cheese
Pizza Sauce
1 (3½-ounce) package sliced pepperoni
1 (8-ounce) can sliced mushrooms, drained
1 small green pepper, cut into strips
1 small onion, sliced and separated into rings
½ cup grated Parmesan cheese

Cook noodles according to package directions; drain. Rinse with cold water, and drain again.

Cover a greased 15- x 10- x 1-inch jellyroll pan with half of noodles, arranging noodles lengthwise in pan, and overlapping sides slightly. (It may be necessary to cut one noodle into smaller pieces to cover pan.)

Sprinkle noodles with half of mozzarella; top with remaining noodles. Spread Pizza Sauce evenly over noodles.

Bake, uncovered, at 375° for 12 minutes. Arrange pepperoni, mushrooms, green pepper, and onion over pizza. Sprinkle with remaining mozzarella and Parmesan cheese. Bake 15 additional minutes. **Yield: 4 to 6 servings.**

Pizza Sauce

1 (8-ounce) can tomato sauce
1 (10¾-ounce) can tomato puree
1 clove garlic, minced
2 teaspoons dried oregano
1 teaspoon dried basil
1 teaspoon dried fennel seeds
¼ teaspoon pepper
⅛ teaspoon salt

Combine all ingredients, mixing well. **Yield: about 2 cups.**

Sausage-Pepperoni Lasagna

1 (8-ounce) package lasagna noodles, uncooked
1 pound ground pork sausage
1 (30-ounce) jar spaghetti sauce
1 large egg, lightly beaten
1 (15-ounce) carton ricotta cheese
1 tablespoon dried parsley flakes
½ teaspoon dried oregano
¼ teaspoon pepper
¼ cup grated Parmesan cheese
2 cups (8 ounces) shredded mozzarella cheese
1 (4.5-ounce) jar sliced mushrooms, drained
1 (3½-ounce) package sliced pepperoni
Garnishes: pepperoni slices, fresh parsley sprigs

Cook lasagna noodles according to package directions, omitting salt; drain.

Brown sausage in a large skillet, stirring until it crumbles; drain. Combine cooked sausage and spaghetti sauce; set aside. Combine egg, ricotta cheese, and next 4 ingredients; set aside.

Spread about ½ cup meat sauce in a lightly greased 13- x 9- x 2-inch baking dish. Layer half of noodles, half of ricotta cheese mixture, one-third of mozzarella cheese, and one-third of remaining meat sauce; repeat layers. Arrange mushrooms and pepperoni slices on top; spoon on remaining sauce.

Bake at 375° for 20 minutes. Sprinkle with remaining mozzarella cheese; bake 5 additional minutes. Let stand 10 minutes before serving. Garnish, if desired. **Yield: 6 to 8 servings.**

Note: To make lasagna ahead, assemble, cover, and refrigerate unbaked casserole 8 hours or overnight. Remove from refrigerator; let stand, covered, 30 minutes. Bake at 375°, uncovered, for 30 minutes; sprinkle with remaining mozzarella cheese. Bake 5 additional minutes; let stand 10 minutes before serving. Garnish, if desired.

Sausage-Pepperoni Lasagna

Tortellini au Gratin

Tortellini au Gratin

¼ pound mild Italian sausage
2 tablespoons finely chopped onion
1 (9-ounce) package refrigerated cheese-filled tortellini, uncooked
3 cloves garlic, unpeeled
½ cup whipping cream
½ cup canned diluted chicken broth
½ cup freshly grated Parmesan cheese, divided
¼ cup plus 2 tablespoons minced fresh parsley, divided
1½ tablespoons minced fresh basil
1 (2-ounce) jar diced pimiento, drained
⅛ teaspoon pepper
2 tablespoons fine, dry breadcrumbs
1½ tablespoons butter or margarine
Garnishes: sliced cherry tomatoes, fresh basil sprigs

Remove and discard casing from sausage. Cook sausage and onion in a skillet over medium heat, stirring until sausage browns and crumbles. Drain well; set aside.

Cook tortellini according to package directions, adding unpeeled cloves of garlic to water. Drain well, reserving garlic. Set tortellini aside; peel and crush garlic.

Combine garlic and whipping cream in a medium bowl; beat with a wire whisk until blended. Add reserved sausage mixture, tortellini, chicken broth, ¼ cup plus 2 tablespoons Parmesan cheese, ¼ cup minced parsley, basil, pimiento, and pepper; stir gently to combine.

Place tortellini mixture in a greased 1-quart baking dish. Combine breadcrumbs and remaining 2 tablespoons minced parsley. Sprinkle over tortellini; dot with butter.

Bake at 325° for 40 minutes. Sprinkle remaining 2 tablespoons Parmesan cheese over breadcrumbs; bake 5 additional minutes or until lightly browned. Garnish, if desired. **Yield: 4 servings.**

Spaghetti alla Carbonara

1 (12-ounce) package spaghetti, uncooked
½ cup whipping cream
3 large eggs, beaten
1 cup grated Parmesan cheese, divided
8 slices bacon, cooked and crumbled
¼ cup butter or margarine
¼ cup chopped fresh parsley
1 clove garlic, crushed
½ teaspoon pepper
⅛ teaspoon dried onion powder
⅛ teaspoon dried basil
⅛ teaspoon dried oregano
1 cup cooked English peas

Cook spaghetti according to package directions, omitting salt. Drain; place in a bowl, and keep warm.

Heat whipping cream in a heavy saucepan over medium heat until hot. Gradually stir about one-fourth of hot cream into eggs; add to remaining cream, stirring constantly. Cook, stirring constantly, 1 minute or until mixture reaches 160°.

Add ½ cup cheese and next 8 ingredients, stirring until butter melts. Pour over spaghetti; add peas, and toss. Sprinkle with remaining ½ cup cheese. **Yield: 4 servings.**

Did You Know?

Carbonara is an Italian term referring to pasta dishes with a white cheese sauce of cream, Parmesan cheese, crumbled bacon, and sometimes eggs. Occasionally, English peas are added for extra color and flavor.

Broccoli-Parmesan Fettuccine

2 cups broccoli flowerets
8 ounces fettuccine, uncooked
2 tablespoons butter or margarine
1 (6-ounce) package Canadian bacon, cut into
    thin strips
⅓ cup whipping cream
1½ cups freshly grated Parmesan cheese
½ teaspoon salt
½ teaspoon freshly ground pepper

Cook broccoli in boiling water to cover 3 minutes; drain and plunge into ice water. Drain and set aside.

Cook fettuccine according to package directions; drain and place in a large bowl. Set aside.

Melt butter in a large skillet over medium-high heat. Add Canadian bacon, and cook, stirring constantly, 2 minutes. Stir in broccoli, and cook 1 minute or until thoroughly heated.

Add broccoli mixture, whipping cream, and remaining ingredients to fettuccine; toss gently. Serve immediately. **Yield: 4 servings.**

Party Pasta with Prosciutto

½ cup butter or margarine, divided
2 cups thin prosciutto strips (about ⅓ pound)
1 (12-ounce) package spinach fettuccine,
    uncooked
1½ cups whipping cream
½ cup freshly grated Parmesan cheese
1 (14-ounce) can artichoke hearts, drained
    and halved
½ cup chopped fresh or frozen chives, divided

Melt ¼ cup butter in a skillet. Add prosciutto, and cook over medium heat until browned, stirring often; drain. Set aside.

Cook pasta according to package directions; drain well.

Melt remaining ¼ cup butter in a Dutch oven over medium heat. Add pasta, whipping cream, cheese, artichoke hearts, and ¼ cup chives; toss gently. Arrange on a serving platter.

Sprinkle with prosciutto and remaining chives. Serve immediately. **Yield: 6 servings.**

Note: If prosciutto is not available, you may substitute cooked, crumbled bacon for the cooked prosciutto.

Pasta with Collards and Sausage

1 pound penne or rigatoni (short tubular
    pasta), uncooked
1 pound spicy smoked sausage, sliced
1 (8-ounce) package sliced fresh mushrooms
2 cloves garlic, minced
3 tablespoons olive oil
2 (10-ounce) packages frozen chopped collard
    greens, thawed and well drained
1 tablespoon dried Italian seasoning
2 (14½-ounce) cans chunky Italian-seasoned
    tomatoes, undrained
Freshly grated Parmesan cheese

Cook pasta according to package directions; drain and set aside.

Brown sausage in a Dutch oven; remove from pan, drain on paper towels, and discard drippings. Set sausage aside.

Cook mushrooms and garlic in olive oil in Dutch oven over medium heat, stirring constantly, until mushrooms are tender. Add sausage, collard greens, Italian seasoning, and tomatoes. Cook 10 minutes.

Add pasta, and toss well. Serve with grated Parmesan cheese. **Yield: 8 servings.**

Poultry Pleasers

Pastas of every twirl, curl, and strand team with poultry for enticing fare. The mild flavors of these two basics are complemented by a variety of seasonings.

Italian Chicken, Taste-of-Texas Pasta and Chicken, Cajun Pasta

Turkey with Tarragon Cream, Pasta and Garden Vegetables, Turkey Noodle Bake

Chicken with Artichokes and Mushrooms, Paprika Chicken, Bird's-Nest Chicken

Chicken and Tomatoes over Fettuccine, Pesto Chicken and Pasta

Turkey-Noodle-Poppy Seed Casserole (page 56)

Italian Chicken

2 pounds chicken breasts, thighs, and legs, skinned
1 (14½-ounce) can tomato wedges, drained
1 (6-ounce) can whole mushrooms, drained
1 (6-ounce) can pitted ripe olives, drained
1 (14-ounce) can artichoke hearts, drained
1 (8-ounce) bottle Italian salad dressing
½ cup dry white wine
1 (1-ounce) envelope onion soup mix
1 (8-ounce) package linguine, uncooked

Place chicken pieces in a lightly greased 13- x 9- x 2-inch baking dish. Arrange tomato wedges, mushrooms, olives, and artichoke hearts on top.

Combine salad dressing and wine; pour over vegetables and chicken. Sprinkle with onion soup mix. Cover and bake at 350° for 1 hour or until chicken is tender.

Cook linguine according to package directions; drain. Remove chicken from baking dish, and set aside.

Stir vegetable mixture, and spoon over linguine on a serving platter. Arrange chicken pieces on top, and serve immediately. **Yield: 4 servings.**

Chicken Paprikash

1 (3-pound) broiler-fryer, cut up
¼ cup butter or margarine, melted
½ cup chopped onion
¼ cup all-purpose flour
2 tablespoons Hungarian paprika
2 cups chicken broth
½ teaspoon salt
¼ teaspoon pepper
1 (8-ounce) carton sour cream
Hot cooked noodles

Brown chicken in butter in a Dutch oven over medium heat. Remove chicken, reserving drippings in Dutch oven; drain on paper towels.

Add onion to drippings; cook over medium heat, stirring constantly, until tender. Add flour and paprika; cook, stirring constantly, 1 minute. Gradually add chicken broth; cook, stirring constantly, until thickened and bubbly. Stir in salt and pepper. Add chicken; cover, reduce heat, and simmer 1 hour or until chicken is tender.

Stir in sour cream; cook, stirring constantly, just until thoroughly heated (do not boil). Serve over noodles. **Yield: 4 servings.**

Chicken with Artichokes and Mushrooms

4 skinned and boned chicken breast halves
¼ cup all-purpose flour
2 tablespoons butter or margarine
1 (14-ounce) can artichoke hearts, drained and quartered
1 (4-ounce) can sliced mushrooms, drained
1 cup whipping cream
½ teaspoon cracked pepper
Hot cooked noodles

Place chicken between 2 sheets of heavy-duty plastic wrap; flatten to ¼-inch thickness, using a meat mallet or rolling pin. Dredge chicken lightly in flour.

Melt butter in a large skillet over medium heat. Add chicken, and cook 5 minutes on each side or until golden; cover and cook 5 minutes. Drain drippings from pan.

Add artichokes and next 3 ingredients to skillet; cook, stirring constantly, over low heat until sauce is thickened. Serve over hot cooked noodles. **Yield: 4 servings.**

From top: Taste-of-Texas Pasta and Chicken and Ravioli with Creamy Pesto Sauce (page 108)

Taste-of-Texas Pasta and Chicken

¼ cup olive oil
1 tablespoon lime juice
⅛ teaspoon ground red pepper
4 skinned and boned chicken breast halves
1 (9-ounce) package refrigerated linguine, uncooked
2 tablespoons butter, melted
1 to 1½ teaspoons grated lime rind
1 tablespoon olive oil
1 clove garlic, crushed
1 (16-ounce) jar mild, thick-and-chunky salsa
Garnish: lime slices

Combine ¼ cup olive oil, lime juice, and red pepper in a heavy-duty zip-top plastic bag; seal and shake well. Add chicken; seal and chill 15 minutes.

Cook pasta according to package directions; drain. Add butter and lime rind; toss well, and keep warm.

Remove chicken from marinade; discard marinade. Heat 1 tablespoon oil in a large skillet over medium heat. Add chicken, and cook 10 to 15 minutes or until tender, turning once. Remove chicken, and set aside.

Add garlic to skillet, and cook, stirring constantly, until lightly browned. Add salsa, and bring to a boil. Arrange pasta and chicken on individual serving plates; top with salsa mixture. Garnish, if desired. **Yield: 4 servings.**

Paprika Chicken

1 tablespoon margarine
4 skinned and boned chicken breast halves
1 (10¾-ounce) can reduced-sodium cream of
    mushroom soup, undiluted
1 tablespoon paprika
½ teaspoon dried tarragon
½ teaspoon salt
½ teaspoon ground red pepper
⅓ cup sour cream
Hot cooked egg noodles
Chopped fresh parsley

Melt margarine in a large nonstick skillet over medium-high heat; add chicken, and cook until browned on both sides.

Combine soup and next 4 ingredients; add to skillet, turning chicken to coat. Cover and cook over medium heat 8 minutes or until chicken is tender.

Remove chicken; keep warm. Stir sour cream into pan drippings, and cook 1 minute.

Place chicken on hot cooked noodles; top with sour cream mixture. Sprinkle with chopped fresh parsley. **Yield: 4 servings.**

Chicken Parmesan

6 skinned and boned chicken breast halves
1 large egg, lightly beaten
¼ cup water
½ cup Italian-seasoned breadcrumbs
½ cup grated Parmesan cheese
3 tablespoons butter or margarine
1 (30-ounce) jar spaghetti sauce
Hot cooked egg noodles
1 cup (4 ounces) shredded mozzarella cheese
2 teaspoons grated Parmesan cheese

Place chicken between 2 sheets of heavy-duty plastic wrap. Flatten chicken to ¼-inch thickness, using a meat mallet or rolling pin.

Combine egg and water in a bowl. Combine breadcrumbs and ½ cup Parmesan cheese in a separate bowl. Dip chicken in egg mixture; dredge in breadcrumb mixture.

Melt butter in a skillet over medium heat; add half of chicken, and cook, turning once, until browned. Repeat procedure.

Return chicken to skillet; add spaghetti sauce. Cover and simmer 10 minutes. Place noodles on platter. Spoon chicken and sauce over noodles; sprinkle with mozzarella and Parmesan cheeses. Cover and let stand until cheeses melt. **Yield: 6 servings.**

Bird's-Nest Chicken

8 nested-style angel hair pasta bundles,
    uncooked
8 skinned and boned chicken breast halves
1 teaspoon salt
½ teaspoon pepper
1 (6-ounce) can sliced mushrooms, drained
1 (10-ounce) package frozen chopped spinach,
    thawed and well drained
1 (10¾-ounce) can cream of chicken soup,
    undiluted
⅔ cup water
3 ounces Monterey Jack cheese, diced
3 ounces Cheddar cheese, diced

Cook angel hair pasta nests according to package directions; drain well, keeping nests intact.

Sprinkle chicken with salt and pepper; arrange in a lightly greased 13- x 9- x 2-inch baking dish. Spoon mushrooms and chopped spinach over chicken. Arrange cooked pasta nests over spinach.

Combine soup and water in a small saucepan; bring to a boil, stirring constantly. Pour sauce evenly over pasta nests. Bake at 375° for 1 hour.

Combine Monterey Jack and Cheddar cheeses; sprinkle over pasta. Bake 5 additional minutes. **Yield: 8 servings.**

Pasta and Garden Vegetables

2 tablespoons butter or margarine
1 tablespoon olive oil
1 pound skinned and boned chicken breasts
   (about 4 breast halves), cut into strips
1½ cups chopped leeks
3 carrots, scraped and sliced
1 sweet red pepper, cut into 1-inch pieces
½ cup chopped onion
¼ cup chopped fresh parsley
2 teaspoons chopped fresh basil
3 small zucchini, diagonally sliced
2 large tomatoes, diced
½ cup chicken broth
½ teaspoon garlic salt
¼ teaspoon pepper
3 cups rotini (corkscrew pasta), uncooked
2 tablespoons freshly grated Parmesan cheese
2 tablespoons freshly grated Romano cheese

Heat butter and olive oil in a large skillet. Add chicken and next 6 ingredients; cover and simmer 10 minutes.

Add zucchini and next 4 ingredients. Cover and cook 10 minutes or until zucchini is crisp-tender.

Cook rotini according to package directions; drain well. Combine pasta and cheeses in a large bowl; stir well to coat. Add vegetables and chicken, stirring to blend. Serve immediately. **Yield: 6 servings.**

Pesto Chicken and Pasta

1 pound skinned and boned chicken breasts
1 tablespoon vegetable oil
1 cup sliced mushrooms
1 (14½-ounce) can tomato wedges, drained
1 cup chicken broth
1 tablespoon cornstarch
3 tablespoons commercial pesto sauce, divided
8 ounces fettuccine, uncooked

Cut chicken into 1-inch pieces, and set aside.

Place a 10-inch browning skillet in microwave oven; preheat, uncovered, at HIGH 6 minutes or according to manufacturer's instructions. Add oil to hot skillet, tilting to coat surface. Add chicken, stirring well. Microwave, uncovered, at HIGH 3 to 4 minutes or until chicken is no longer pink, stirring every 2 minutes.

Stir in mushrooms and tomato wedges; microwave at HIGH 4 to 5 minutes or until mushrooms are tender.

Combine chicken broth and cornstarch; stir until smooth. Add to chicken mixture; microwave at HIGH 5 to 6 minutes or until slightly thickened. Add 1 tablespoon pesto sauce, stirring well.

Cook fettuccine according to package directions; drain. Combine hot fettuccine and remaining pesto sauce, tossing gently. Serve chicken mixture over pasta. **Yield: 4 servings.**

Cooking Tip

When cooking long pasta shapes (spaghetti, fettuccine, linguine, and angel hair), it's not necessary to break the pasta into shorter pieces. Hold one end of the pasta by the handful, and set the other end in boiling water, pushing pasta gently until it softens enough to submerge.

Cajun Pasta

Cajun Pasta

1½ cups water
½ pound unpeeled medium-size fresh shrimp
2 skinned and boned chicken breast halves, cut into ¼-inch strips
½ pound andouille or Cajun smoked sausage, sliced
½ cup chopped onion
1 clove garlic, minced
1 tablespoon olive oil
½ cup dry white wine
½ cup chicken broth
1 teaspoon all-purpose flour
1 cup whipping cream
1 tablespoon Cajun or Creole seasoning
2 tablespoons tomato paste
1 teaspoon cracked pepper (optional)
1 green pepper, cut into thin strips
1 sweet red pepper, cut into thin strips
1 (16-ounce) package fettuccine, uncooked

Bring water to a boil; add shrimp, and cook 3 to 5 minutes or until shrimp turn pink. Drain; rinse with cold water. Peel shrimp, and devein, if desired. Set aside.

Cook chicken and next 3 ingredients in olive oil in a large skillet over medium-high heat, stirring often, until meat is lightly browned; remove chicken mixture from skillet, and set aside.

Add wine to skillet. Bring to a boil; reduce heat, and simmer 3 to 5 minutes or until wine is reduced to ¼ cup.

Combine chicken broth and flour, stirring until smooth. Add chicken broth mixture, whipping cream, Cajun seasoning, tomato paste, and if desired, cracked pepper to skillet. Bring to a boil. Reduce heat, and simmer 20 minutes.

Add chicken mixture and pepper strips; cook until thoroughly heated. Keep warm.

Cook fettuccine according to package directions; drain. Combine fettuccine and chicken mixture; toss gently. **Yield: 6 to 8 servings.**

Chicken-Vegetable Spaghetti

4 skinned and boned chicken breast halves, cut into 2-inch strips
2 tablespoons olive oil
3 medium zucchini, cut in half lengthwise and sliced (about 1 pound)
1 large green pepper, coarsely chopped
½ pound fresh mushrooms, sliced
¼ cup chopped onion
1 clove garlic, minced
1 (30-ounce) jar spaghetti sauce
2 cups (8 ounces) shredded mozzarella cheese, divided
8 to 12 ounces spaghetti, uncooked
2 tablespoons chopped fresh parsley

Cook chicken in hot oil in a large skillet, stirring constantly, until no longer pink. Drain and set aside, reserving 1 tablespoon drippings in skillet.

Add zucchini and next 4 ingredients to skillet; cook over medium heat, stirring constantly, until crisp-tender. Stir in chicken and spaghetti sauce; cook until thoroughly heated, stirring occasionally. Stir in 1 cup mozzarella cheese; cook until cheese melts, stirring often.

Cook spaghetti according to package directions; drain. Arrange spaghetti on a large platter, and top with sauce mixture. Sprinkle with remaining 1 cup cheese and parsley. Serve immediately. **Yield: 4 to 6 servings.**

Chicken and Tomatoes over Fettuccine

1 (7-ounce) jar oil-packed dried tomatoes, undrained
6 ounces fettuccine, uncooked
½ cup chopped onion
2 cloves garlic, minced
4 skinned and boned chicken breast halves, cut into strips
3 tablespoons chopped fresh basil or 1 tablespoon dried basil
¼ teaspoon salt
¼ teaspoon pepper

Drain tomatoes, reserving oil. Coarsely chop tomatoes; set aside.

Cook fettuccine according to package directions, omitting salt. Drain and keep warm.

Heat 1 tablespoon reserved oil from tomatoes in a large skillet. Cook onion and garlic in hot oil until tender. Add chicken, and cook, stirring constantly, 8 minutes or until tender.

Add basil and reserved tomatoes to skillet; cook 2 minutes. Stir in salt, pepper, and 2 tablespoons reserved oil from tomatoes.

Place fettuccine on a large platter. Spoon chicken mixture over fettuccine, and toss well. **Yield: 4 servings.**

Try Fresh Basil

Fresh basil, an herb often used in tomato-based pasta dishes, is usually available at supermarkets. To preserve its delicate flavor in long-cooking dishes, add basil near the end of cooking time. Basil bruises easily, so handle it carefully. Cut it with a sharp, thin-bladed stainless-steel knife, or chop it in a food processor using a few 3- to 5-second pulses.

Pasta-Chicken Potpourri

4 ounces penne (short tubular pasta), uncooked
1 teaspoon sesame oil
1½ tablespoons olive oil
1½ tablespoons sesame oil
2 medium carrots, scraped and diagonally sliced
1 small purple onion, chopped
2 medium zucchini, halved lengthwise and sliced
2 cloves garlic, crushed
1½ teaspoons grated fresh ginger
½ teaspoon dried crushed red pepper
2 cups chopped cooked chicken
2 tablespoons soy sauce
2 teaspoons rice wine vinegar
Freshly grated Parmesan cheese

Cook penne pasta according to package directions; drain and toss with 1 teaspoon sesame oil. Set pasta aside.

Pour olive oil and 1½ tablespoons sesame oil around top of preheated wok or large skillet, coating sides; heat at medium-high (375°) for 2 minutes.

Add carrot and onion to wok; stir-fry 3 minutes. Add zucchini and next 3 ingredients; stir-fry 1 minute.

Stir in pasta, chicken, soy sauce, and vinegar; stir-fry 1 minute or until thoroughly heated. Transfer to a serving dish; sprinkle with Parmesan cheese. **Yield: 4 servings.**

Pasta-Chicken Potpourri

Chicken Fettuccine

Chicken Fettuccine

½ pound fresh mushrooms, sliced
1 small sweet red pepper, cut into thin strips
1 small onion, chopped
1 clove garlic, crushed
2 tablespoons butter or margarine, melted
3 cups chopped cooked chicken
1 (8-ounce) package fettuccine, uncooked
½ cup whipping cream
½ cup butter or margarine
½ cup grated Parmesan cheese
2 tablespoons chopped fresh parsley
¼ teaspoon ground white pepper

Cook first 4 ingredients in 2 tablespoons butter in a large skillet over medium heat, stirring constantly, until vegetables are tender. Add chicken, and cook until thoroughly heated. Set aside, and keep warm.

Cook fettuccine according to package directions; drain and place in a large bowl.

Combine whipping cream and ½ cup butter in a small saucepan; cook over low heat until butter melts. Stir in Parmesan cheese, parsley, and white pepper.

Pour whipping cream mixture over hot fettuccine; add chicken mixture. Toss until fettuccine is thoroughly coated. **Yield: 6 to 8 servings.**

Chicken Lasagna Florentine

6 lasagna noodles, uncooked
1 (10-ounce) package frozen chopped spinach, thawed
2 cups chopped cooked chicken
2 cups (8 ounces) shredded Cheddar cheese
⅓ cup finely chopped onion
¼ to ½ teaspoon freshly ground nutmeg
1 tablespoon cornstarch
½ teaspoon salt
¼ teaspoon pepper
1 tablespoon soy sauce
1 (10¾-ounce) can cream of mushroom soup, undiluted
1 (8-ounce) carton sour cream
1 (4.5-ounce) jar sliced mushrooms, drained
⅓ cup mayonnaise or salad dressing
1 cup freshly grated Parmesan cheese
Butter-Pecan Topping

Cook noodles according to package directions; drain and set aside.

Drain spinach well, pressing between layers of paper towels.

Combine spinach, chicken, and next 11 ingredients in a large bowl; stir well to blend.

Arrange 2 noodles in a lightly greased 11- x 7- x 1½-inch baking dish. Spread half of chicken mixture over noodles. Repeat procedure, and top with remaining 2 lasagna noodles. Sprinkle with Parmesan cheese and Butter-Pecan Topping.

Cover and bake at 350° for 55 to 60 minutes or until hot and bubbly. Let stand 15 minutes before cutting. **Yield: 8 servings.**

Butter-Pecan Topping

2 tablespoons butter or margarine
1 cup chopped pecans

Melt butter in a skillet over medium heat; add pecans, and cook 3 minutes. Cool completely. **Yield: 1 cup.**

Ravioli with Parmesan Sauce

3 tablespoons minced shallots or onion
3 tablespoons butter, melted
¾ pound fresh mushrooms, finely chopped
2 teaspoons minced garlic
¾ cup plus 2 tablespoons whipping cream, divided
½ cup diced cooked chicken
¼ cup finely chopped prosciutto
¾ teaspoon chopped fresh thyme
⅔ cup ricotta cheese
1¾ cups plus 3 tablespoons grated Parmesan cheese, divided
2 egg yolks, beaten
3 cups all-purpose flour
1½ teaspoons salt, divided
3 large eggs
1 tablespoon vegetable oil
1 to 2 tablespoons water
⅓ cup butter
⅓ cup all-purpose flour
2½ cups milk
4 quarts water
½ cup butter, melted
Chopped fresh parsley
Additional chopped fresh thyme

Cook shallots in 3 tablespoons butter 1 minute. Add mushrooms and garlic; cook until liquid evaporates, stirring constantly. Add ¼ cup plus 2 tablespoons whipping cream; cook over medium heat, stirring until liquid is absorbed.

Stir in chicken, prosciutto, and ¾ teaspoon thyme; cool. Stir in ricotta cheese, 3 tablespoons Parmesan cheese, and egg yolks; chill.

Combine 3 cups flour and 1 teaspoon salt; make a well in center. Combine 3 eggs, oil, and 1 tablespoon water; beat well. Add to flour mixture, stirring until blended. Add remaining 1 tablespoon water, if necessary.

Turn dough out onto a floured surface, and knead until smooth and elastic. Cover; let rest 10 minutes.

Divide dough into fourths. Working with one portion at a time (keep unused portions covered), pass dough through pasta machine, starting at widest setting. Continue moving width gauge to narrower settings, passing dough through twice at each setting until about 1/16-inch thick, 6 inches wide, and 48 inches long.

Place one strip of dough on a floured surface. Cut lengthwise into 2-inch-wide strips. Top with about 1½ teaspoons filling at 2-inch intervals. Moisten with water around filling; top with second strip. Press with fingertips to seal. Cut between filling into 2-inch squares. Let dry on a towel 1 hour, turning once. Repeat procedure.

Melt ⅓ cup butter over low heat. Add ⅓ cup flour; stir until smooth. Cook, stirring constantly, 1 minute.

Add milk and remaining ½ cup whipping cream; cook over medium heat, stirring constantly, until thickened and bubbly. Stir in 1½ cups Parmesan cheese; keep sauce warm.

Bring 4 quarts water and remaining ½ teaspoon salt to a boil in a Dutch oven; add half of ravioli at a time, and cook 10 to 12 minutes. Drain. Dip in ½ cup melted butter. Place in a single layer on baking sheets; sprinkle with remaining ¼ cup Parmesan cheese. Broil 6 inches from heat 3 minutes or until golden. Serve with sauce; sprinkle with herbs. **Yield: 6 to 8 servings.**

Ravioli Technique

Working with one portion at a time, pass ravioli dough through rollers of pasta machine.

Ravioli with Parmesan Sauce

Quick Chicken and Pasta

2 quarts water
½ teaspoon salt
4 ounces vermicelli, uncooked
¾ cup frozen English peas
⅓ cup Italian salad dressing
1 cup chopped cooked chicken
¼ teaspoon sweet red pepper flakes
2 tablespoons grated Parmesan cheese

Combine water and salt in a large saucepan; bring to a boil. Add vermicelli and peas. Return water to a boil; reduce heat, and cook 10 minutes. Drain and set aside.

Heat salad dressing in saucepan. Add chicken and red pepper flakes; cook, stirring constantly, 2 minutes.

Add pasta mixture, and cook until thoroughly heated. Sprinkle with Parmesan cheese, tossing mixture well. **Yield: 2 servings.**

Chicken Lasagna

1 (2½- to 3-pound) broiler-fryer
6 cups water
1 teaspoon salt
1 clove garlic, minced
2 tablespoons butter, melted
1 (10¾-ounce) can cream of celery soup, undiluted
½ teaspoon dried oregano
¼ teaspoon pepper
8 lasagna noodles, uncooked
1 (8-ounce) loaf process American cheese, cut in ¼-inch slices, divided
2 cups (8 ounces) shredded mozzarella cheese, divided
2 tablespoons grated Parmesan cheese

Place chicken in a Dutch oven; add water and salt, and bring to a boil. Cover, reduce heat, and simmer 45 minutes or until tender. Drain, reserving broth, and let cool slightly.

Remove chicken from bone, cutting meat into bite-size pieces; set aside.

Cook garlic in butter in a skillet over medium-high heat, stirring constantly, 2 minutes. Add soup, ¾ cup reserved chicken broth, oregano, and pepper.

Cook lasagna noodles according to package directions in remaining reserved chicken broth, adding more water, if necessary; drain.

Spoon a small amount of sauce into a lightly greased 11- x 7- x 1½-inch baking dish. Layer with half each of noodles, sauce, chicken, and American and mozzarella cheeses. Repeat procedure with noodles, sauce, and chicken, reserving remaining cheeses.

Bake at 350° for 25 minutes; top with remaining cheeses, and bake 5 additional minutes. Let stand 10 minutes. **Yield: 6 servings.**

Turkey-Noodle-Poppy Seed Casserole

(pictured on page 43)

1 (8-ounce) package medium-size egg noodles, uncooked
½ cup chopped onion
¼ cup chopped green pepper
¼ cup butter or margarine, melted
3 tablespoons all-purpose flour
3 cups milk
¼ cup grated Parmesan cheese
1 tablespoon poppy seeds
1 teaspoon salt
⅛ teaspoon ground red pepper
3 cups diced cooked turkey
1 (4-ounce) jar diced pimiento, drained
2 tablespoons grated Parmesan cheese

Cook noodles according to package directions. Drain and set aside.

Cook onion and green pepper in butter in a Dutch oven until tender; add flour, stirring until smooth. Cook, stirring constantly, 1 minute.

Add milk; cook over medium heat, stirring constantly, until thickened and bubbly. Stir in noodles, ¼ cup Parmesan cheese, and next 5 ingredients.

Spoon mixture into a lightly greased 13- x 9- x 2-inch baking dish. Cover and chill 8 hours. To bake, remove from refrigerator, and let stand 30 minutes. Bake, covered, at 350° for 45 minutes. Uncover and sprinkle with 2 tablespoons Parmesan cheese. Bake, uncovered, 10 additional minutes or until thoroughly heated. **Yield: 6 to 8 servings.**

Note: Unbaked casserole may be frozen. To bake, thaw in refrigerator 24 hours. Remove from refrigerator, and let stand 30 minutes. Bake, covered, at 350° for 45 minutes. Uncover, and sprinkle with 2 tablespoons cheese. Bake, uncovered, 10 additional minutes or until thoroughly heated.

Microwave Directions:

Prepare casserole as directed in a microwave-safe baking dish; cover and chill 8 hours. Remove from refrigerator, and let stand 30 minutes.

Shield corners of casserole with microwave-safe aluminum foil. Cover baking dish tightly with heavy-duty plastic wrap; fold back a small corner of wrap to allow steam to escape.

Microwave at MEDIUM (50% power) 10 minutes, stirring after 5 minutes. Microwave at HIGH 20 minutes, stirring after 10 minutes.

Uncover and remove shield; sprinkle with 2 tablespoons cheese, and microwave at HIGH 3 minutes.

Note: To microwave frozen casserole, remove from freezer, and shield corners with microwave-safe aluminum foil.

Cover tightly with heavy-duty plastic wrap; fold back a small corner of wrap to allow steam to escape.

Microwave at MEDIUM 30 minutes, stirring after 15 minutes. Microwave at HIGH 10 to 12 minutes, stirring after 5 minutes.

Uncover and remove shield; sprinkle with 2 tablespoons cheese, and microwave at HIGH 3 minutes.

Herbed Turkey Tetrazzini

¼ **cup chopped onion**
¼ **cup chopped fresh mushrooms**
¼ **cup butter or margarine, melted**
¼ **cup all-purpose flour**
1 **cup milk**
1 **cup chicken broth**
½ **cup (2 ounces) shredded Swiss or Gruyère
    cheese, divided**
1 **tablespoon chopped fresh parsley**
1 **teaspoon dried tarragon**
⅛ **teaspoon pepper**
Dash of ground nutmeg
2½ **cups cooked spaghetti or fettuccine**
1½ **cups chopped cooked turkey**
Garnishes: chopped parsley, red pepper strips

Cook onion and mushrooms in butter in a large, heavy saucepan, stirring constantly, until just tender. Add flour; cook, stirring constantly, 1 minute.

Add milk and chicken broth; cook over medium heat, stirring constantly, until mixture is thickened and bubbly.

Stir in ¼ cup cheese, parsley, and next 5 ingredients, mixing well.

Spoon into a greased 1½-quart baking dish. Bake at 350° for 20 minutes. Sprinkle remaining ¼ cup cheese over top, and bake 5 additional minutes. Garnish, if desired. **Yield: 4 servings.**

Turkey Noodle Bake

Turkey with Tarragon Cream

1 pound cooked turkey breast
2 tablespoons butter or margarine, divided
1 tablespoon all-purpose flour
¾ cup milk
2 tablespoons chopped fresh parsley
½ teaspoon dried tarragon
½ cup sour cream
1 tablespoon Dijon mustard
Hot cooked noodles

Cut turkey into ¼-inch slices. Melt 1 tablespoon butter in a large skillet; add turkey slices, and cook 2 minutes on each side. Arrange turkey on a platter; keep warm.

Melt remaining tablespoon butter in skillet over low heat; add flour, stirring constantly. Gradually add milk; cook over medium heat, stirring constantly, until thickened and bubbly. Remove from heat.

Stir in parsley and next 3 ingredients. Pour sauce over turkey slices. Serve over noodles. **Yield: 4 servings.**

Turkey Noodle Bake

2 pounds ground turkey or beef
2 cups chopped celery
¼ cup chopped green pepper
¼ cup chopped onion
2 tablespoons olive oil
1 (10¾-ounce) can cream of mushroom soup, undiluted
¼ cup soy sauce
1 (8-ounce) can sliced water chestnuts, drained
1 (4.5-ounce) jar sliced mushrooms, drained
1 (4-ounce) jar chopped pimiento, drained
1 teaspoon salt
½ teaspoon lemon-pepper seasoning
1 (5-ounce) package egg noodles, uncooked
1 (8-ounce) carton sour cream
¼ cup sliced almonds, toasted
Garnish: celery leaves

Cook first 4 ingredients in olive oil in a Dutch oven over medium heat until meat crumbles, stirring often. Drain. Stir in mushroom soup and next 6 ingredients. Bring to a boil; cover, reduce heat, and simmer 20 minutes, stirring often.

Cook noodles according to package directions; drain. Stir noodles and sour cream into turkey mixture; divide in half.

Spoon mixture into 2 lightly greased 2-quart shallow baking dishes; bake at 350° for 20 minutes or until heated. Top with almonds, and garnish, if desired. **Yield: 4 servings per casserole.**

Note: To freeze Turkey Noodle Bake, line two 2-quart shallow baking dishes with aluminum foil; set aside. Assemble casseroles as directed, and spoon into prepared dishes; freeze. Frozen casseroles may be removed from baking dishes. Wrap in foil, or place in large heavy-duty plastic freezer bags; freeze up to 6 months.

Remove foil, and place frozen casserole in a lightly greased 2-quart shallow baking dish. Cover and bake at 350° for 1 hour and 30 minutes. Top with almonds, and garnish, if desired.

Seafood Sensations

Catch the pasta wave with these delicious pasta and seafood combinations. From clams to shrimp, these pairings are appropriate for family fare or entertaining.

Linguine with Red Clam Sauce, Crawfish Lasagna, Dilled Shrimp

Angel Hair Pasta with Shrimp and Asparagus, Shrimp-and-Vegetable Spaghetti

Scallop Kabobs with Saffron Orzo, Herbed Shrimp and Pasta, Scallops in Wine

Creamy Shrimp and Noodles, Shrimp Scampi, Salmon Fettuccine

Garlic-Buttered Shrimp (page 72)

Linguine with Red Clam Sauce

8 cloves garlic, sliced in half
3 bay leaves, divided
2 tablespoons olive oil
1 cup chopped onion
3 (6½-ounce) cans minced clams, undrained
2 (15-ounce) cans tomato sauce
1 (6-ounce) can tomato paste
½ cup chicken broth
½ cup dry white wine
1½ teaspoons dried basil
1 teaspoon salt
1 teaspoon dried thyme
½ teaspoon ground red pepper
½ teaspoon black pepper
¼ teaspoon ground white pepper
1 (16-ounce) package linguine, uncooked
⅓ cup chopped fresh parsley (optional)

Cook garlic and 2 bay leaves in olive oil in a large saucepan over medium heat 2 minutes, stirring often. Remove and mince 1 tablespoon garlic, discarding any remaining garlic; return minced garlic to saucepan.

Add onion, and cook 6 minutes or until tender and browned, stirring frequently.

Drain clams, reserving 1 cup clam juice; discard remaining juice. Set clams aside. Add reserved clam juice, remaining bay leaf, tomato sauce, and next 9 ingredients to onion mixture. Bring to a boil.

Cover, reduce heat, and simmer 20 minutes, stirring occasionally.

Cook linguine according to package directions; drain and set aside.

Add clams to sauce; simmer 5 minutes. Discard bay leaves. Place linguine on a warm platter; top with sauce. Sprinkle with chopped parsley, if desired. **Yield: 6 to 8 servings.**

Red Clam Sauce Techniques

Cook garlic and bay leaves in olive oil until garlic is golden. The oil takes on a subtle garlic flavor.

Drain canned clams, reserving 1 cup juice. Use clam juice to flavor tomato sauce.

Simmer red clam sauce until thickened. Discard bay leaves before spooning sauce over hot cooked linguine.

Linguine with Red Clam Sauce

Clam Linguine

Clam Linguine

8 ounces linguine, uncooked
2 tablespoons butter
1 clove garlic, minced
2 tablespoons all-purpose flour
1 tablespoon chopped fresh oregano or
   1 teaspoon dried oregano
2 (10-ounce) cans whole clams, undrained
½ cup dry white wine
¼ cup whipping cream
¼ cup grated Parmesan cheese

Cook linguine according to package directions; drain and keep warm.

Melt butter in a large skillet over medium heat; add garlic, and cook, stirring constantly, 1 minute. Add flour and oregano; cook, stirring constantly, 1 minute.

Stir in clams and wine; cook, stirring constantly, 8 minutes or until mixture reduces slightly. Remove from heat.

Stir in whipping cream, and cook over low heat until thoroughly heated. Spoon over linguine; sprinkle with cheese. **Yield: 4 servings.**

Linguine with Clam Sauce

8 ounces linguine, uncooked
2 (6½-ounce) cans minced clams, undrained
½ medium onion, chopped
¼ cup olive oil
1 tablespoon chopped fresh parsley
½ teaspoon garlic powder

Cook linguine in a Dutch oven according to package directions. Drain; return to Dutch oven. Set aside. Drain clams, reserving liquid; set aside.

Cook onion in olive oil in a medium saucepan until tender. Add reserved clam liquid, and simmer 15 minutes. Stir in clams, parsley, and garlic powder. Heat thoroughly.

Add clam mixture to linguine, tossing well. Cook until mixture is thoroughly heated. Serve immediately. **Yield: 4 servings.**

Seafood and Pasta

2 cups sliced fresh mushrooms
¾ cup chopped onion
¼ cup butter or margarine, melted
1 (10¾-ounce) can cream of mushroom soup,
   undiluted
1 cup half-and-half
2 tablespoons grated Parmesan cheese
¼ teaspoon garlic salt
½ teaspoon dried parsley flakes
1 (16-ounce) package refrigerated crab-
   flavored seafood product, chopped
Hot cooked shell macaroni

Cook mushrooms and onion in butter in a large skillet over medium heat, stirring constantly, until tender.

Add mushroom soup and next 5 ingredients. Cook over medium heat, stirring constantly, until thoroughly heated. Serve over shell macaroni. **Yield: 4 servings.**

Seafood Manicotti

2 pounds unpeeled large fresh shrimp
1 quart whipping cream
½ teaspoon salt
¼ teaspoon ground black pepper
¼ teaspoon ground red pepper
14 manicotti shells, uncooked
1 cup chopped onion
1 cup chopped green pepper
¼ cup chopped celery
1 clove garlic, minced
3 tablespoons butter or margarine, melted
1 pound fresh crabmeat, drained and flaked
½ cup (2 ounces) shredded Cheddar cheese
½ cup (2 ounces) shredded Monterey Jack
   cheese with peppers

Peel shrimp, and devein, if desired. Chop and set aside.

Combine whipping cream and next 3 ingredients in a heavy saucepan; cook over medium-high heat 30 minutes or until thickened and reduced to 2 cups. Set aside.

Cook manicotti according to package directions; drain and set aside.

Cook onion and next 3 ingredients in butter in a large Dutch oven over medium-high heat, stirring constantly, 5 minutes or until tender.

Add shrimp and crabmeat, and cook, stirring constantly, 5 minutes or until shrimp turn pink. Cool 10 minutes, and drain well.

Combine seafood mixture and whipping cream mixture.

Fill manicotti shells, and place in 2 lightly greased 11- x 7- x 1½-inch baking dishes. Sprinkle filled shells with cheeses, and cover with aluminum foil.

Bake at 350° for 15 minutes. Uncover and bake 10 additional minutes. Serve immediately.
Yield: 6 to 8 servings.

Crawfish Stroganoff

1 medium onion, chopped
1 medium-size green pepper, seeded and
   chopped
1 tablespoon vegetable oil
¼ cup butter or margarine
⅓ cup all-purpose flour
⅔ cup water
1 pound fresh or frozen peeled crawfish tails
½ teaspoon salt
½ teaspoon pepper
1 (8-ounce) carton sour cream
Hot cooked noodles

Cook onion and green pepper in hot oil in a large skillet, stirring constantly, until tender. Remove from skillet, and set aside.

Melt butter in skillet over low heat; add flour, stirring until smooth. Cook, stirring constantly, 1 minute. Gradually add water; cook over medium heat, stirring constantly, until mixture is thickened and bubbly. Add vegetables, crawfish, salt, and pepper; cover and simmer 30 minutes.

Remove from heat, and stir in sour cream. Cook over medium heat until thoroughly heated. (Do not boil.) Serve over hot cooked noodles.
Yield: 4 servings.

Did You Know?

Many cooks use a flavored seafood product called surimi instead of "real" crabmeat or lobster. Inexpensive whitefish is transformed to imitate the texture, shape, and flavor of crabmeat, shrimp, lobster, or scallops. This seafood product is rich in protein, low in fat and cholesterol, fully cooked, and ready to eat when purchased.

Crawfish Lasagna

1 cup chopped onion
¾ cup chopped celery
¾ cup chopped green pepper
⅓ cup butter or margarine, melted
3 cloves garlic, minced
1 teaspoon dried basil
1 teaspoon dried oregano
¼ teaspoon salt
¼ teaspoon pepper
Dash of hot sauce
½ teaspoon liquid crab boil
⅓ cup all-purpose flour
3 cups milk
1 (8-ounce) carton sour cream
4 cups (16 ounces) shredded Monterey Jack
    cheese, divided
2 pounds fresh or frozen peeled crawfish tails
⅔ cup chopped green onions
⅓ cup chopped fresh parsley
1 teaspoon dried oregano
1 teaspoon dried basil
½ teaspoon salt
½ teaspoon pepper
Dash of hot sauce
9 lasagna noodles, uncooked
½ teaspoon liquid crab boil
1 tablespoon vegetable oil

Crawfish filling for Crawfish Lasagna

Cook first 3 ingredients in butter in a Dutch oven over medium heat, stirring constantly, until tender. Add garlic and next 6 ingredients.

Add flour, stirring until smooth. Cook, stirring constantly, 1 minute. Gradually add milk; cook over medium heat, stirring constantly, until mixture is thickened and bubbly.

Whisk in sour cream and 3 cups cheese, stirring until smooth.

Cook crawfish tails and green onions in a skillet over medium heat until thoroughly heated; drain. Stir into white sauce; add parsley and next 5 ingredients. Simmer over low heat 5 to 6 minutes.

Cook lasagna noodles according to package directions, adding ½ teaspoon crab boil and oil to water; drain.

Place half of noodles in a lightly greased 13- x 9- x 2-inch baking dish. Layer half of sauce over noodles; repeat layers.

Bake at 350° for 40 minutes. Sprinkle with remaining 1 cup cheese, and bake 5 additional minutes. Let lasagna stand 10 minutes before serving. **Yield: 10 to 12 servings.**

Mussels Linguine

2 pounds raw mussels in shells
3 tablespoons olive oil
½ cup chopped fresh parsley
5 cloves garlic, minced
2 tablespoons dry white wine
1 (15½-ounce) jar spaghetti sauce
½ teaspoon dried oregano
⅛ teaspoon freshly ground pepper
8 ounces linguine, uncooked

Remove beards on mussels, and scrub mussel shells well with a brush. Discard opened, cracked, or heavy mussels.

Combine oil, parsley, and garlic in an 11- x 7- x 1½-inch baking dish; microwave at HIGH, uncovered, 3 to 5 minutes. Stir in wine, spaghetti sauce, oregano, and pepper.

Arrange mussels over sauce in a single layer. Cover tightly with heavy-duty plastic wrap; fold back a corner of wrap to allow steam to escape. Microwave at HIGH 6 to 7 minutes or until mussels open.

Cook linguine according to package directions; drain. Place cooked linguine on a platter; top with mussels and sauce. **Yield: 4 servings.**

Salmon-Pesto Vermicelli

1 cup firmly packed fresh basil leaves
¼ cup commercial Italian dressing
2 tablespoons water
3 cloves garlic, crushed
1 (1-pound) salmon fillet
¼ teaspoon cracked pepper
Vegetable cooking spray
1 (8-ounce) package vermicelli, cooked
6 lemon wedges (optional)

Combine first 4 ingredients in a food processor bowl fitted with knife blade. Process 2 minutes,
scraping sides of bowl occasionally. Set aside.

Sprinkle fish with pepper, and place, skin side down, on a broiler pan coated with cooking spray.

Broil 6 inches from heat (with electric oven door partially opened) 5 minutes. Carefully turn over, and broil 4 additional minutes or until fish flakes easily when tested with a fork.

Remove fish from pan; cool. Remove and discard skin; break fish into bite-size pieces.

Combine fish, basil mixture, and vermicelli in a large bowl; toss gently. Serve with lemon wedges, if desired. **Yield: 4 to 6 servings.**

Salmon Fettuccine

8 ounces fettuccine, uncooked
1½ tablespoons butter or margarine
1½ tablespoons all-purpose flour
2 cups half-and-half
1 cup freshly grated Parmesan cheese
1½ teaspoons dry sherry
¼ teaspoon salt
¼ teaspoon ground white pepper
1 clove garlic, minced
2 tablespoons butter or margarine, melted
½ pound salmon fillet, cut into 2-inch pieces

Cook fettuccine according to package directions; drain and set aside.

Melt 1½ tablespoons butter in a heavy saucepan over low heat; add flour, stirring until smooth. Cook, stirring constantly, 1 minute.

Add half-and-half; cook over medium heat, stirring constantly, until mixture is thickened and bubbly. Stir in cheese, sherry, salt, and pepper. Keep warm.

Cook garlic in 2 tablespoons butter in a large skillet. Add salmon; cook until fish begins to flake. Add sauce and fettuccine, tossing gently. Cook over low heat just until thoroughly heated. Serve immediately. **Yield: 4 servings.**

Scallop Kabobs with Saffron Orzo

1 (15¼-ounce) can pineapple chunks,
    undrained
½ cup dry white wine
½ cup soy sauce
¼ cup lemon juice
2 tablespoons olive oil
2 tablespoons chopped fresh parsley
1 teaspoon pepper
½ teaspoon garlic powder
1 pound fresh sea scallops
2 medium-size green peppers, seeded and cut
    into 1-inch squares
12 medium-size fresh mushrooms
12 cherry tomatoes
1 cup dry white wine
1 cup water
2 teaspoons chicken-flavored bouillon
    granules
¼ teaspoon ground saffron
1 cup orzo (rice-shaped pasta), uncooked

Drain pineapple, reserving juice. Set pineapple aside. Combine pineapple juice, ½ cup wine, and next 6 ingredients in a bowl; stir well. Remove half of marinade mixture, and chill.

Place remaining marinade in a large shallow dish. Add pineapple, scallops, green pepper, mushrooms, and tomatoes; toss gently to coat evenly. Cover and chill 1 hour.

Combine 1 cup wine, water, bouillon granules, and saffron in a medium saucepan; stir well. Bring to a boil over medium heat. Add orzo; return to a boil.

Cover, reduce heat to medium-low, and simmer 10 to 12 minutes or until orzo is tender. Drain, if necessary. Set aside, and keep warm.

Drain scallop mixture; discard marinade. Alternate pineapple, scallops, green pepper, mushrooms, and tomatoes on 6 (12-inch) metal skewers.

Cook kabobs 4 to 5 inches from medium-hot coals (350° to 400°) 10 to 12 minutes or until

scallops are done, turning and basting frequently with reserved marinade. Arrange orzo on a serving platter. Serve kabobs over warm orzo. **Yield: 6 servings.**

Scallop Kabobs Techniques

Add pineapple, scallops, and vegetables to marinade; cover and chill 1 hour.

Alternate pineapple chunks, scallops, green pepper, mushrooms, and tomatoes on 12-inch skewers.

Place saffron-flavored orzo on a serving platter, and arrange kabobs over orzo.

Scallop Kabobs with Saffron Orzo

Scallops in Wine

1 pound fresh bay scallops
¼ cup butter or margarine, melted
½ cup sliced fresh mushrooms
¼ cup chopped onion
1 clove garlic, minced
½ cup dry white wine
3 tablespoons lemon juice
3 tablespoons lime juice
½ teaspoon dried oregano
½ teaspoon celery salt
¼ teaspoon pepper
Hot cooked vermicelli
Garnish: chopped fresh parsley

Cook scallops in butter in a large skillet over medium heat, stirring constantly, 3 minutes or until tender. Remove scallops from skillet, reserving drippings.

Cook mushrooms, onion, and garlic, stirring constantly, 3 to 5 minutes in skillet; remove vegetables, reserving drippings.

Add wine and next 5 ingredients to skillet. Bring to a boil, and cook 8 minutes.

Stir in scallops and vegetables; cook until thoroughly heated. Serve over hot vermicelli, and garnish, if desired. **Yield: 3 to 4 servings.**

Shrimp Scampi

1 pound unpeeled medium-size fresh shrimp
8 ounces angel hair pasta, uncooked
4 cloves garlic, minced
½ cup butter or margarine, melted
⅓ cup dry white wine
¼ teaspoon freshly ground pepper
¾ cup (3 ounces) grated Romano cheese
1 tablespoon chopped fresh parsley

Peel shrimp, and devein, if desired; set aside.
Cook pasta according to package directions;

drain and place on a large serving platter, and keep warm.

Cook shrimp and garlic in butter in a large skillet over medium heat, stirring constantly, 3 to 5 minutes or until shrimp turn pink; add wine and pepper. Bring to a boil; cook, stirring constantly, 30 seconds.

Pour shrimp mixture over pasta; sprinkle with cheese and parsley, and toss gently. Serve immediately. **Yield: 4 servings.**

Creamy Shrimp and Noodles

1 pound unpeeled medium-size fresh shrimp
6 ounces fettuccine, uncooked
1 small sweet red pepper, cut into strips
2 tablespoons butter or margarine, melted
1¼ cups milk
2 (0.6-ounce) envelopes cream of chicken-flavored instant soup mix
½ cup frozen English peas
3 tablespoons grated Parmesan cheese
¼ teaspoon garlic powder

Peel shrimp, and devein, if desired; set aside.
Cook fettuccine according to package directions; drain and set aside.

Cook shrimp and red pepper in butter in a large skillet over medium-high heat, stirring constantly, 3 minutes or until shrimp turn pink.

Combine milk and soup mix; add to shrimp mixture. Stir in peas, cheese, and garlic powder.

Bring to a boil; reduce heat and simmer, stirring often, 5 minutes or until thickened. Toss shrimp mixture with fettuccine. Serve immediately. **Yield: 3 to 4 servings.**

Herbed Shrimp and Pasta

Herbed Shrimp and Pasta

1 pound unpeeled medium-size fresh shrimp
4 ounces angel hair pasta, uncooked
2 cloves garlic, minced
½ cup butter, melted
1 cup half-and-half
¼ cup chopped fresh parsley
1 teaspoon chopped fresh dill or ½ teaspoon
    dried dillweed
¼ teaspoon salt
⅛ teaspoon pepper
Steamed pepper strips

Peel shrimp, and devein, if desired; set aside.
Cook pasta according to package directions.

Drain and set aside; keep warm.

Cook shrimp and garlic in butter in a heavy skillet over medium-high heat, stirring constantly, 3 to 5 minutes or until shrimp turn pink. Remove shrimp, and set aside, reserving garlic and butter in skillet.

Add half-and-half to skillet; bring to a boil, stirring constantly. Reduce heat to low, and simmer about 15 minutes or until thickened, stirring occasionally. Add shrimp, parsley, and seasonings; stir until blended.

Serve shrimp over steamed or sautéed red, green, and yellow pepper strips and angel hair pasta. **Yield: 2 to 3 servings.**

Dilled Shrimp

Dilled Shrimp

2 pounds unpeeled large fresh shrimp
½ cup butter or margarine
⅓ cup chopped green onions
2 large cloves garlic, crushed
1 tablespoon lemon juice
1 tablespoon chopped fresh dill or 1 teaspoon
    dried dillweed
1 (2-ounce) jar diced pimiento, drained
3 cups hot cooked medium egg noodles
2 tablespoons butter or margarine
Salt and pepper to taste
Garnish: fresh dill sprigs

Peel shrimp, and devein, if desired; set aside.

Combine ½ cup butter, green onions, and garlic in a 13- x 9- x 2-inch baking dish. Cover tightly with heavy-duty plastic wrap; fold back a small corner of wrap to allow steam to escape.

Microwave at HIGH 1 to 2 minutes or until butter melts and green onions are tender. Add shrimp and lemon juice, stirring to coat.

Cover and microwave at HIGH 4 minutes, stirring after 2 minutes. Stir in chopped dill.

Cover and microwave at HIGH 1 to 3 minutes or until shrimp turn pink. Let stand, covered, 1 minute. Stir in pimiento.

Combine hot cooked noodles, 2 tablespoons butter, salt, and pepper; stir until butter melts. Arrange noodles on a serving platter. Top with shrimp mixture. Garnish, if desired. **Yield: 6 servings.**

Angel Hair Pasta with Shrimp and Asparagus

8 unpeeled jumbo fresh shrimp
4 ounces angel hair pasta, uncooked
¼ cup olive oil
2 tablespoons minced garlic
1 teaspoon chopped shallots
6 stalks asparagus, cut into 2-inch pieces
¼ cup diced, seeded, and peeled tomato
½ cup sliced shiitake mushroom caps
¼ teaspoon salt
⅛ teaspoon dried crushed red pepper
½ cup dry white wine
1 tablespoon chopped fresh basil
1 tablespoon chopped fresh oregano
1 tablespoon chopped fresh thyme
1 tablespoon chopped fresh parsley
¼ cup freshly grated Parmesan cheese

Peel shrimp, and devein, if desired; set aside.

Cook pasta according to package directions; drain and set aside.

Heat a 9-inch skillet over high heat 1 minute; add oil, and heat 10 seconds. Add shrimp, garlic, and shallots; cook, stirring constantly, 2 to 3 minutes or until shrimp turn pink.

Add asparagus and next 4 ingredients; stir in wine, scraping bottom of skillet to loosen any particles, if necessary. Add pasta, basil, and remaining ingredients; toss gently. Serve immediately. **Yield: 2 servings.**

Note: You may substitute ½ cup sliced fresh mushrooms for shiitake mushrooms.

Shrimp and Pasta

Shrimp and Pasta

1½ pounds unpeeled medium-size fresh
    shrimp
1 (12-ounce) package spaghetti, uncooked
1 tablespoon Old Bay seasoning
1 cup broccoli flowerets
1 clove garlic, minced
3 tablespoons olive oil
1 bunch green onions, chopped
1 (4-ounce) can sliced mushrooms, drained
1 (4-ounce) can sliced water chestnuts,
    drained
½ cup sour cream
Grated Parmesan cheese

Peel shrimp, and devein, if desired; set aside.

Cook spaghetti according to package directions, omitting salt and adding Old Bay seasoning. Drain and return to Dutch oven; keep warm.

Cook broccoli and garlic in olive oil in a large skillet, stirring constantly, 3 to 4 minutes. Add green onions; cook 1 minute. Add shrimp, and cook, stirring constantly, 4 minutes.

Stir in mushrooms and water chestnuts; cook until thoroughly heated. Stir in sour cream; heat thoroughly, but do not boil.

Serve over spaghetti; sprinkle with Parmesan cheese. **Yield: 6 servings.**

Garlic-Buttered Shrimp

(pictured on page 59)

2 pounds unpeeled large fresh shrimp
½ cup butter or margarine
½ cup olive oil
¼ cup minced fresh parsley
1 tablespoon plus 1½ teaspoons lemon juice
1 green onion, minced
3 cloves garlic, minced
¼ teaspoon coarsely ground black pepper
8 ounces linguine, uncooked

Peel and devein shrimp, leaving tails intact (tails may be removed, if desired). Set aside.

Place butter in a 13- x 9- x 2-inch baking dish. Microwave, uncovered, at HIGH 1 minute or until melted. Stir in olive oil and next 5 ingredients; arrange shrimp around outer edges of baking dish.

Cover tightly with heavy-duty plastic wrap, and marinate in refrigerator at least 1 hour.

Remove from refrigerator. Fold back a small corner of wrap to allow steam to escape, and microwave at HIGH 7 to 7½ minutes or until shrimp turn pink, rearranging shrimp every 2 minutes.

Cook linguine according to package directions; drain and place on a serving platter. Top pasta with shrimp mixture. Serve immediately.
Yield: 6 servings.

Shrimp with Pasta Primavera

3 pounds unpeeled medium-size fresh shrimp
1½ cups chopped green onions
3 to 4 cloves garlic, minced
¾ teaspoon salt
¾ teaspoon ground red pepper
¾ teaspoon black pepper
¾ teaspoon dried basil
¾ teaspoon dried oregano
¾ teaspoon dried thyme
1½ cups butter or margarine, melted
1½ pounds fresh mushrooms, sliced
1 cup dry white wine
Pasta Primavera
Garnishes: cherry tomatoes, fresh parsley
    sprigs

Peel shrimp, and devein, if desired; set aside.

Cook green onions and next 7 ingredients in butter in a large skillet over medium heat, stirring often.

Add shrimp, mushrooms, and wine; cook 3 to 4 minutes or until shrimp turn pink, stirring occasionally. Remove from skillet with a slotted spoon, and serve over Pasta Primavera. Garnish, if desired. **Yield: 12 servings.**

Pasta Primavera

2 (12-ounce) packages thin spaghetti or
    vermicelli, uncooked
1 (8-ounce) bottle red wine-and-vinegar salad
    dressing
3 medium-size green peppers, seeded and
    chopped
3 medium-size sweet red peppers, seeded and
    chopped
3 medium-size yellow squash, cut into thin
    strips
1½ cups chopped green onions
¾ cup sliced pitted ripe olives
½ teaspoon salt

Cook spaghetti according to package directions; drain and keep warm.

Combine salad dressing and remaining 6 ingredients in a large skillet; cook over medium heat about 5 minutes or until vegetables are crisp-tender, stirring often. Pour over spaghetti, tossing gently. **Yield: 12 servings.**

Artichoke-and-Shrimp Linguine

1 pound unpeeled medium-size fresh shrimp
8 ounces linguine, uncooked
3 cloves garlic, minced
½ teaspoon dried crushed red pepper
¼ cup olive oil
1 (14-ounce) can artichoke hearts, drained
    and quartered
½ cup ripe olives, sliced
¼ cup fresh lemon juice
⅛ teaspoon salt
⅛ teaspoon pepper
½ cup grated Parmesan cheese

Peel shrimp, and devein, if desired; set aside.

Cook linguine according to package directions; drain and keep warm.

Cook shrimp, garlic, and red pepper in hot oil in a skillet over medium-high heat, stirring constantly, 5 minutes or until shrimp turn pink.

Stir in artichoke hearts and next 4 ingredients. Add to pasta, and sprinkle with cheese. **Yield: 3 to 4 servings.**

Shrimp-and-Fish Lasagna

6 lasagna noodles, uncooked
3 tablespoons vegetable oil, divided
6 cups water
1 pound unpeeled medium-size fresh shrimp
1 large onion, chopped
1 (3-ounce) package cream cheese, softened
1 cup cottage cheese
1 teaspoon Italian seasoning
½ teaspoon salt
¼ teaspoon coarsely ground pepper
⅛ teaspoon salt-free herb-and-spice blend
Dash of ground nutmeg
1 large egg, beaten
1 (10-ounce) package frozen chopped spinach,
    thawed and drained
1 (10¾-ounce) can cream of celery soup,
    undiluted
⅓ cup evaporated skim milk
4 flounder fillets (about 1 pound), cut into
    1-inch pieces
1 pound crabmeat or crab-flavored seafood
    product
2 tablespoons lemon juice
3 tablespoons grated Parmesan cheese
3 tablespoons seasoned, dry breadcrumbs
2 tablespoons butter or margarine, melted
⅓ cup (1.33 ounces) shredded Cheddar cheese

Cook noodles according to package directions, adding 1 tablespoon vegetable oil to boiling water; drain. Arrange noodles in a lightly greased 13- x 9- x 2-inch baking dish. Set aside.

Bring water to a boil; add shrimp, and partially cook 1 minute. Drain well; rinse with cold water. Peel shrimp, and devein, if desired; set aside.

Cook onion in remaining 2 tablespoons oil in a large skillet over medium heat, stirring constantly, until translucent.

Add cream cheese and next 7 ingredients to skillet; cook over medium-low heat until cheese is blended, stirring occasionally. Stir in spinach; spoon over lasagna noodles.

Combine shrimp, soup, and next 4 ingredients; stir well. Spoon over spinach mixture.

Combine Parmesan cheese, breadcrumbs, and butter; sprinkle over lasagna.

Bake at 350° for 45 minutes. Sprinkle with Cheddar cheese, and bake 5 additional minutes or until cheese melts. Remove from oven, and let stand 15 minutes before cutting. **Yield: 8 servings.**

Shrimp-and-Vegetable Spaghetti

1 pound unpeeled medium-size fresh shrimp
4 slices bacon
1 cup chopped onion
1 medium-size green pepper, seeded and
    chopped
4 carrots, scraped and sliced diagonally
¼ teaspoon garlic powder
2 (14.5-ounce) cans whole tomatoes,
    undrained and chopped
1 (2.25-ounce) can sliced ripe olives, drained
1 teaspoon dried basil
1 teaspoon dried oregano
¼ teaspoon pepper
¼ teaspoon garlic salt
8 ounces fresh mushrooms, sliced
Hot cooked vermicelli
Grated Parmesan cheese

Peel shrimp, and devein, if desired; set aside.

Cook bacon in a large skillet until crisp; remove bacon, reserving 1 tablespoon drippings in skillet. Crumble bacon, and set aside.

Cook onion and next 3 ingredients in bacon drippings until carrot is crisp-tender. Add tomatoes and next 5 ingredients; bring to a boil. Cover, reduce heat, and simmer 3 to 5 minutes.

Add shrimp and mushrooms; cook 10 minutes. Serve over vermicelli; sprinkle with bacon and cheese. **Yield: 6 servings.**

Vegetable Variations

For a special luncheon dish or a spur-of-the-moment gathering, team pasta with garden-fresh vegetables. This collection combines pasta with everything from artichokes to zucchini.

Black Bean Spaghetti, Bow Tie Pesto, Caribbean Tomato Pasta

Pasta with Greens, Peppery Pasta, Spinach-Stuffed Manicotti, Vegetable Lasagna

Super-Quick Pasta, Pasta with Peppers and Broccoli, Spaghetti with Vegetables

Orzo Primavera, Pasta Primavera, Linguine with Grilled Vegetables

Roasted Vegetables and Pasta (page 86)

Super-Quick Pasta

Super-Quick Pasta

2½ cups ziti (short tubular pasta), uncooked
2 cups commercial spaghetti sauce
1 cup ricotta cheese
⅛ teaspoon salt
¼ teaspoon pepper
¼ cup chopped fresh parsley
½ cup (2 ounces) shredded mozzarella cheese
Garnish: fresh parsley sprigs

Cook pasta according to package directions; drain and set aside.

Cook spaghetti sauce in a saucepan over medium heat 10 to 12 minutes, stirring occasionally. Remove from heat, and set aside.

Combine pasta, ricotta cheese, salt, and pepper; spoon onto individual serving plates. Stir chopped parsley into spaghetti sauce, and spoon over pasta mixture. Sprinkle with mozzarella cheese, and serve immediately. Garnish, if desired. **Yield: 4 servings.**

Note: For variation, add 1 (14-ounce) can artichoke hearts, drained and quartered, or 1 cup steamed zucchini slices to the spaghetti sauce.

Bow Tie Pesto

1 (16-ounce) package bow tie pasta, uncooked
2 cups tightly packed fresh basil
1½ cups freshly grated Parmesan cheese
1 (1¾-ounce) jar pine nuts
3 cloves garlic, halved
⅔ cup olive oil
1 (14-ounce) can artichoke hearts, drained and quartered
½ cup oil-packed dried tomatoes, drained and cut into thin strips

Cook pasta according to package directions; drain and set aside.

Position knife blade in food processor bowl; add basil and next 3 ingredients. Process until smooth, stopping once to scrape down sides.

Pour olive oil through food chute with processor running; process until smooth. Set pesto mixture aside.

Place pasta in a large bowl. Add 1½ cups pesto mixture and artichoke hearts. (Reserve remaining pesto mixture for another use.)

Sprinkle pasta with tomatoes, and serve hot or cold. **Yield: 8 servings.**

Caribbean Tomato Pasta

3 large vine-ripened tomatoes
¾ cup canned black beans, drained and rinsed
2 tablespoons extra-virgin olive oil
3 cloves garlic, minced
2 tablespoons chopped fresh cilantro
1 tablespoon chopped fresh chives
1 tablespoon fresh lime juice
½ teaspoon ground cumin
¼ teaspoon ground red pepper
¼ teaspoon salt
¼ teaspoon black pepper
4 ounces vermicelli, uncooked
½ cup (2 ounces) shredded Monterey Jack cheese

Peel tomatoes, and coarsely chop over a medium bowl, reserving juice. Combine chopped tomato, reserved juice, beans, and next 9 ingredients; cover and let stand at room temperature at least 1 hour.

Cook pasta according to package directions; drain. Serve tomato mixture over pasta, and sprinkle with cheese. **Yield: 2 servings.**

Black Bean Spaghetti

Black Bean Spaghetti

1 large onion, sliced
1 small sweet red pepper, cut into strips
1 small sweet yellow pepper, cut into strips
1 (8-ounce) package fresh mushrooms, sliced
2 tablespoons olive oil
1 (16-ounce) can whole tomatoes, undrained
    and chopped
1 (15-ounce) can black beans, drained and
    rinsed
1 (15½-ounce) can kidney beans, undrained
1 (3½-ounce) jar capers, undrained
¼ cup sliced ripe olives
¼ teaspoon dried rosemary
¾ teaspoon chopped fresh basil or
    ¼ teaspoon dried basil
¼ teaspoon pepper
Hot cooked angel hair pasta
Freshly grated Parmesan cheese
Garnish: fresh basil leaves

Cook first 4 ingredients in olive oil in a large skillet over medium-high heat, stirring constantly, until tender.

Add tomatoes and next 7 ingredients; bring to a boil. Reduce heat, and simmer 30 minutes, stirring occasionally.

Serve over pasta, and sprinkle with Parmesan cheese. Garnish, if desired. **Yield: 6 servings.**

Spaghetti with Vegetables

1 cup sliced fresh mushrooms
¾ cup chopped onion
3 cloves garlic, minced
6 large fresh basil leaves, chopped
¼ teaspoon finely ground fennel seeds
¼ cup plus 3 tablespoons olive oil, divided
1½ cups broccoli flowerets
1½ cups cauliflower flowerets
1 (15½-ounce) can red kidney beans, rinsed
    and drained
¼ to ½ teaspoon salt
2 quarts water
1 teaspoon salt
1 (7-ounce) package spaghetti, uncooked
½ cup freshly grated Parmesan cheese
Freshly ground pepper

Cook first 5 ingredients in 2 tablespoons olive oil, stirring constantly, 3 to 4 minutes or until onion is tender; remove from skillet.

Add 3 tablespoons olive oil to skillet, and cook broccoli and cauliflower, stirring constantly, 5 minutes or until crisp-tender. Add onion mixture, beans, and ¼ to ½ teaspoon salt to vegetables; heat thoroughly. Set aside, and keep warm.

Combine water, 1 tablespoon olive oil, and 1 teaspoon salt; bring to a boil, and add spaghetti. Cook spaghetti 10 to 13 minutes, stirring occasionally. Drain. Add remaining 1 tablespoon olive oil to spaghetti, tossing to coat.

Combine cooked spaghetti, vegetable mixture, and cheese in a large serving bowl, tossing well. Top with freshly ground pepper. **Yield: 6 to 8 servings.**

Pasta with Greens

1 (8-ounce) package fettuccine, uncooked
1 (16-ounce) package frozen collards or other greens
2 to 3 cloves garlic, minced
3 tablespoons olive oil
½ teaspoon salt
¼ teaspoon freshly ground pepper
½ cup freshly grated Parmesan cheese
1 (1¾-ounce) jar pine nuts, toasted
Garnishes: grated Parmesan cheese, toasted pine nuts

Cook pasta according to package directions; drain and set aside.

Cook greens according to package directions; drain and set aside.

Cook garlic in olive oil in a large skillet over medium-high heat until tender but not brown. Add greens, salt, and pepper; cook until heated.

Combine pasta, greens, Parmesan cheese, and pine nuts in a large serving bowl. Garnish, if desired. **Yield: 2 servings.**

Pasta with Greens

Pasta Potpourri

4 ounces penne or rigatoni (short tubular pasta), uncooked
1 teaspoon sesame oil
1½ tablespoons olive oil
1½ tablespoons sesame oil
1 small purple onion, chopped
2 medium carrots, scraped and diagonally sliced
2 medium zucchini, halved lengthwise and sliced
2 cloves garlic, crushed
1½ teaspoons peeled, grated gingerroot
½ teaspoon dried crushed red pepper
2 tablespoons soy sauce
2 teaspoons rice wine vinegar
1 tablespoon freshly grated Parmesan cheese
2 teaspoons chopped fresh cilantro

Cook pasta according to package directions; drain and toss with 1 teaspoon sesame oil. Set pasta aside.

Pour olive oil and 1½ tablespoons sesame oil around top of a preheated wok, coating sides; heat at high 1 minute. Add onion and carrot; cook, stirring constantly, 2 minutes or until onion is tender.

Add zucchini and next 3 ingredients; cook, stirring constantly, 1 minute.

Stir in cooked pasta, soy sauce, and vinegar; cook 1 minute or until thoroughly heated.

Transfer to a serving dish; sprinkle with cheese and cilantro. **Yield: 4 to 6 servings.**

Note: For a quick main dish, add leftover chopped cooked chicken or beef.

Peppery Pasta

3 pounds ripe plum tomatoes, peeled and
    quartered
8 green onions, thinly sliced
8 cloves garlic, minced
1 tablespoon olive oil
2 small sweet banana peppers, thinly sliced
⅓ cup chopped fresh oregano or
    2 tablespoons dried oregano
¼ cup chopped fresh basil or 1½ teaspoons
    dried basil
½ teaspoon salt
8 green onions, thinly sliced
3 sweet yellow peppers, cut into thin strips
3 sweet red or orange peppers, cut into thin
    strips
3 tablespoons chopped fresh oregano or
    1 tablespoon dried oregano
1 tablespoon olive oil
10 to 12 crimini or button mushrooms,
    coarsely chopped
1 teaspoon salt
1 teaspoon dried crushed red pepper
1 pound hot cooked mostaccioli (tubular
    pasta)
8 ounces fontina or mozzarella cheese,
    shredded

Position knife blade in food processor bowl;
add one-third of tomato. Pulse 5 or 6 times or
until finely chopped. Remove tomato from bowl,
and set aside. Repeat procedure twice.

Cook 8 green onions and garlic in 1 tablespoon olive oil in a large, heavy saucepan, stirring constantly, 10 minutes or until tender.

Stir in tomato, banana pepper, and next 3
ingredients.

Bring mixture to a boil over medium heat,
stirring constantly; reduce heat, and simmer,
uncovered, 1 hour, stirring occasionally. Remove
from heat; keep tomato mixture warm.

Cook 8 green onions, sweet pepper strips, and
3 tablespoons fresh oregano in 1 tablespoon olive
oil in a large skillet over medium heat, stirring
constantly, 12 to 15 minutes or until vegetables
are crisp-tender. Add mushrooms, 1 teaspoon
salt, and crushed red pepper; cook about 7 minutes or until mushrooms are tender, stirring often.

Place hot cooked pasta on a large serving platter.

Pour tomato mixture over pasta; spoon mushroom mixture over sauce, and sprinkle with
shredded cheese. **Yield: 8 servings.**

Pasta with Peppers and Broccoli

1 pound fresh broccoli
1 (7.5-ounce) jar roasted peppers, drained
    and cut into strips
⅔ cup pine nuts
½ cup olive oil
½ cup chopped fresh parsley
1 (12-ounce) package small shell pasta,
    uncooked
1 cup freshly grated Parmesan cheese
⅛ teaspoon black pepper
⅛ teaspoon ground red pepper

Trim off large leaves of broccoli, and remove
tough ends of lower stalks. Wash broccoli thoroughly, and cut into flowerets. Set aside.

Cook roasted peppers and next 3 ingredients
in a skillet over medium heat until nuts are gold-
en, stirring often.

Cook pasta according to package directions,
adding broccoli the last 2 minutes; drain.

Add roasted pepper mixture, cheese, and
remaining ingredients to pasta. Toss and serve
immediately. **Yield: 6 servings.**

Pasta Primavera

Pasta Primavera

1 pound fresh asparagus
2 cups fresh broccoli flowerets
1 medium onion, chopped
1 large clove garlic, chopped
1 tablespoon olive oil
1 large carrot, scraped and diagonally sliced
1 sweet red pepper, coarsely chopped
1 sweet yellow pepper, coarsely chopped
1 cup whipping cream
½ cup chicken broth
3 green onions, chopped
2 tablespoons chopped fresh basil or
    2 teaspoons dried basil
½ teaspoon salt
8 ounces linguine, uncooked
½ pound fresh mushrooms, sliced
1 cup freshly grated Parmesan cheese
¼ teaspoon freshly ground pepper

Snap off tough ends of asparagus. Remove scales with a vegetable peeler or knife, if desired. Cut asparagus diagonally into 1½-inch pieces.

Place asparagus pieces and broccoli flowerets in a vegetable steamer over boiling water. Cover; steam 6 to 8 minutes. Set aside.

Cook onion and garlic in oil in a large skillet, stirring constantly, until tender. Add carrot and chopped peppers; cook, stirring constantly, until crisp-tender. Remove from heat; drain.

Combine whipping cream and next 4 ingredients in a medium skillet; cook over medium-high heat 5 minutes, stirring occasionally.

Break linguine noodles in half; cook according to package directions. Drain well; place in a large serving bowl.

Add reserved vegetables, whipping cream mixture, and mushrooms; toss gently. Sprinkle with Parmesan cheese and pepper; toss gently. Serve immediately. **Yield: 8 servings.**

Orzo Primavera

3 quarts water
1 teaspoon salt
2 cups orzo (rice-shaped pasta), uncooked
1 pound fresh asparagus, cut into 1-inch
    pieces
3 cloves garlic, minced
½ cup chopped sweet red pepper
1 teaspoon butter or margarine, melted
1 tablespoon olive oil
1 cup frozen English peas, thawed
½ cup chicken broth
1 teaspoon grated lemon rind
¼ teaspoon ground white pepper
½ cup freshly grated Parmesan cheese

Combine water and salt in a large Dutch oven; bring to a boil. Add orzo, and cook 5 minutes. Add asparagus, and cook 4 minutes. Drain and set aside in a large serving bowl.

Cook garlic and red pepper in butter and oil in Dutch oven over medium heat, stirring constantly, 1 minute or until crisp-tender. Add peas; cook, stirring constantly, 1 minute. Add broth, lemon rind, and white pepper; bring to a boil, and cook 1 minute.

Add vegetable mixture to orzo mixture, tossing well. Sprinkle with Parmesan cheese. Serve immediately. **Yield: 6 to 8 servings.**

Note: Orzo can be served as a substitute for rice, cooked in soups and stews, or used as the main ingredient in pasta salads.

Garden Spiral Primavera

8 ounces vegetable-flavored rotini (corkscrew pasta), uncooked
2 tablespoons olive oil
¼ cup butter or margarine
1 small onion, thinly sliced
1 clove garlic, minced
1½ cups broccoli flowerets
1 carrot, scraped and sliced
4 ounces fresh mushrooms, sliced
3 tablespoons white wine
1½ teaspoons chopped fresh basil or
    ½ teaspoon dried basil
1½ teaspoons chopped fresh parsley or
    ½ teaspoon dried parsley flakes
¼ teaspoon ground white pepper
½ cup grated Parmesan cheese

Cook pasta according to package directions; drain and set aside.

Heat olive oil and butter in a large skillet; add onion and garlic. Cook over medium heat 2 minutes, stirring frequently. Add broccoli and carrot; cook 2 minutes. Add mushrooms, and cook 1 minute, stirring occasionally.

Add wine, basil, parsley, and pepper; bring to a boil. Cover, reduce heat, and simmer 3 minutes or until vegetables are tender.

Add vegetables and Parmesan cheese to cooked pasta, stirring well. Serve immediately. **Yield: 4 servings.**

Linguine with Grilled Vegetables

2 yellow squash, cut into chunks
2 zucchini, cut into chunks
1 purple onion, quartered
1 small eggplant, unpeeled and cut into chunks
1 sweet red pepper, cut into 1-inch pieces
⅓ cup butter or margarine
2 to 3 teaspoons dried Italian seasoning
½ teaspoon black pepper
2 teaspoons chicken-flavored bouillon granules
2 quarts water
8 ounces linguine, uncooked
¼ cup grated Parmesan cheese

Place first 5 ingredients on a lightly greased 24- x 18-inch piece of heavy-duty aluminum foil; dot with butter, and sprinkle with Italian seasoning and pepper. Seal securely.

Cook on a grill rack over hot coals (400° to 500°) 20 to 30 minutes or until vegetables are tender. Remove from heat, and keep sealed.

Combine bouillon granules and about 2 quarts water in a stockpot; cover and place in hot coals. Bring to a boil; add linguine, and cook until tender. Drain. Top with vegetables; sprinkle with cheese. **Yield: 2 to 3 servings.**

Note: Linguine may be prepared on a conventional cooktop. Cook in bouillon-flavored water according to package directions.

Serving Tip

Serving long, thin pastas such as linguine or fettuccine can be tricky. You may use kitchen tongs or a special wooden pasta fork to transfer the pasta (see page 82). This long-handled fork has 1-inch dowels protruding from the flat surface. These allow you to grab the pasta easily and lift it to plates.

Linguine with Grilled Vegetables

Roasted Vegetables and Pasta

(pictured on page 75)

6 ounces rigatoni (short tubular pasta), uncooked
1 (1-ounce) package onion soup mix
2 teaspoons dried thyme
½ cup olive oil, divided
2 carrots, cut into 1-inch slices
1 medium zucchini, cut into 1-inch slices
1 eggplant, cut into 1-inch pieces
½ pound fresh mushrooms, halved
¼ cup white wine vinegar
⅓ cup pine nuts, toasted
Freshly ground pepper

Cook pasta according to package directions, omitting salt and fat. Drain. Rinse and drain again; place in a large bowl, and set aside.

Combine onion soup mix and thyme; stir in ¼ cup olive oil. Add carrot and next 3 ingredients, tossing to coat.

Spread vegetables evenly into a 15- x 10- x 1-inch jellyroll pan. Bake at 450° for 25 minutes, stirring after 15 minutes. Stir into pasta.

Combine remaining ¼ cup olive oil, white wine vinegar, and pine nuts; pour over pasta mixture, tossing to coat. Sprinkle with pepper. Serve immediately. **Yield: 4 to 6 servings.**

To Serve a Frozen Casserole

Most lasagna and manicotti dishes may be covered and frozen up to 4 months. For best results, prepare the recipe, and freeze it before baking. To serve, thaw in refrigerator 24 hours, and bake as recipe directs.

Thaw Vegetable Lasagna, and bake at 375° for 45 minutes; add remaining mozzarella cheese, and bake 5 minutes.

Vegetable Lasagna

12 lasagna noodles, uncooked
2 cups sliced mushrooms
1 cup shredded carrot (about 5 medium carrots)
½ cup chopped onion
1 tablespoon vegetable oil
1 (18-ounce) can tomato paste
1 (15-ounce) can tomato sauce
1 (4-ounce) can sliced ripe olives, drained
1½ teaspoons dried oregano
1 teaspoon dried fennel
2 cups cottage cheese, divided
1 (10-ounce) package frozen chopped spinach, thawed and well drained
2 (8-ounce) packages sliced mozzarella cheese, divided
Grated Parmesan cheese

Cook noodles according to package directions; drain and set aside.

Cook mushrooms, carrot, and onion in oil in a large skillet over medium heat until tender. Stir in tomato paste and next 4 ingredients; bring to a boil. Remove from heat.

Lightly grease two 8-inch square baking dishes; arrange 3 noodles in each dish. Layer one-fourth each of cottage cheese, spinach, vegetable mixture, and mozzarella in each dish. Repeat layers with remaining noodles, cottage cheese, spinach, and vegetable mixture.

Cover and freeze one casserole up to four months. (To serve frozen casserole, see box at left.) Bake remaining casserole at 375° for 30 minutes. Add half of remaining mozzarella slices, and bake 5 additional minutes. Let casserole stand 10 minutes; serve with Parmesan cheese. **Yield: 4 servings per casserole.**

Note: Vegetable Lasagna may be prepared in a 13- x 9- x 2-inch baking dish. Bake at 375° for 40 minutes; top with remaining mozzarella cheese slices, and bake 5 additional minutes.

Vegetable Lasagna

Lasagna Florentine

2 chicken-flavored bouillon cubes
¼ cup water
½ cup butter or margarine
⅓ cup all-purpose flour
⅛ teaspoon salt
⅛ teaspoon dried Italian seasoning
Dash of garlic powder
Dash of ground nutmeg
¼ teaspoon ground white pepper
¼ teaspoon lemon-pepper seasoning
1 cup whipping cream
1 cup half-and-half
¾ cup chopped onion
1 tablespoon butter or margarine, melted
2 (10-ounce) packages frozen chopped
    spinach, thawed
1 large egg, lightly beaten
1½ cups (6 ounces) shredded mozzarella
    cheese
1 (8-ounce) carton sour cream
9 lasagna noodles, uncooked
½ teaspoon salt
½ cup grated Parmesan cheese

Dissolve bouillon cubes in water; set aside.
Melt ½ cup butter in a heavy saucepan over low
heat. Add flour and next 6 ingredients, stirring
until smooth. Cook, stirring constantly, 1 minute.

Add bouillon mixture, whipping cream, and
half-and-half to flour mixture; cook over medium
heat, stirring until thickened and bubbly. Remove
from heat; set aside.

Cook onion in 1 tablespoon butter until tender.
Drain spinach well by pressing between layers of
paper towels.

Combine spinach, onion, egg, mozzarella
cheese, and sour cream in a large bowl; stir well,
and set mixture aside.

Cook lasagna noodles according to package
directions, adding ½ teaspoon salt; drain.

Layer 3 noodles in a lightly greased 13- x 9- x
2-inch baking dish. Spread with spinach mixture;
repeat with 3 noodles. Spread with half of cream
sauce; repeat with remaining noodles. Spread
with remaining cream sauce; sprinkle with
Parmesan cheese.

Bake, uncovered, at 350° for 30 minutes.
Yield: 6 servings.

Jumbo Shells Florentine

12 jumbo pasta shells, uncooked
1 (10-ounce) package chopped spinach,
    thawed and uncooked
1 small onion, minced
1 large egg, beaten
½ teaspoon salt
⅛ teaspoon pepper
1 cup well-drained cottage cheese
1 (10¾-ounce) can cream of mushroom soup,
    undiluted
⅓ cup water

Cook pasta shells according to package directions; drain and set aside.

Combine spinach, onion, egg, salt, pepper,
and cottage cheese; stir gently.

Spoon spinach mixture into pasta shells, and
place shells in a lightly greased shallow baking
dish. Combine soup and water; pour over shells.

Cover and bake at 350° for 25 minutes. Spoon
sauce over shells, and bake 20 additional minutes.
Yield: 3 main-dish or 6 side-dish servings.

Pasta Stuffed with Five Cheeses

(pictured on cover)

20 jumbo pasta shells, uncooked
1 (8-ounce) package cream cheese, softened
1 cup low-fat cottage cheese
1 cup (4 ounces) shredded mozzarella cheese
1 large egg, lightly beaten
¼ cup grated Parmesan and Romano cheese
    blend
2 tablespoons chopped fresh parsley
2 teaspoons dried basil
½ teaspoon dried oregano
½ teaspoon dried thyme
⅛ teaspoon grated lemon rind
Pinch of ground nutmeg
1 (14½-ounce) can stewed tomatoes,
    undrained
1 (6-ounce) can tomato paste
1 (8-ounce) can tomato sauce
½ cup dry white wine
1 (8-ounce) can mushroom stems and pieces,
    drained
1 teaspoon dried oregano
1 teaspoon dried thyme
1 clove garlic, minced
Garnish: fresh herb sprigs

Cook pasta shells according to package directions; drain and set aside.

Combine cream cheese and next 10 ingredients, mixing well. Stuff jumbo shells with cheese mixture.

Arrange stuffed shells in a lightly greased 13- x 9- x 2-inch baking dish. Cover and bake at 350° for 25 minutes or until thoroughly heated.

Place tomatoes in container of an electric blender or food processor; cover and process until smooth. Pour puree into a Dutch oven; stir in tomato paste and next 6 ingredients.

Bring mixture to a boil; reduce heat, and simmer, uncovered, 20 minutes or until thickened.

Spoon sauce onto serving plates; arrange pasta shells on sauce. Garnish, if desired. **Yield: 4 servings.**

Spinach-Stuffed Manicotti

12 manicotti shells, uncooked
2 (10-ounce) packages frozen chopped
    spinach, thawed and well drained
2 cups (8 ounces) shredded mozzarella cheese
2 cups cottage cheese
½ cup grated Parmesan cheese
1 small onion, diced
2 tablespoons dried parsley flakes
1 teaspoon dried oregano
Dash of hot sauce
Dash of ground nutmeg
1 (32-ounce) jar spaghetti sauce with
    mushrooms, divided
¼ cup grated Parmesan cheese

Cook manicotti shells according to package directions; drain and set aside.

Combine spinach and next 8 ingredients, stirring well. Stuff manicotti shells with spinach mixture.

Spoon 1 cup spaghetti sauce into a lightly greased 13- x 9- x 2-inch baking dish. Arrange stuffed shells over sauce. Spoon remaining sauce over shells; sprinkle with ¼ cup Parmesan cheese.

Cover tightly with aluminum foil, and bake at 350° for 45 minutes or until thoroughly heated. **Yield: 6 servings.**

Spinach-Stuffed Lasagna Ruffles

1 (8-ounce) package lasagna noodles, uncooked
1 (8-ounce) package cream cheese, softened
2 (10-ounce) packages frozen chopped spinach, thawed and drained
1½ cups freshly grated Parmesan cheese, divided
1 (15-ounce) carton ricotta cheese
2 cups (8 ounces) shredded mozzarella cheese
1½ teaspoons dried Italian seasoning
¼ teaspoon salt
1 (32-ounce) jar spaghetti sauce
Garnishes: fresh basil sprigs, grated Parmesan cheese

Cook noodles according to package directions; drain and set aside.

Beat cream cheese until smooth. Stir in spinach, 1 cup Parmesan cheese, and next 4 ingredients.

Spread ½ cup cheese mixture evenly over each cooked noodle. Roll noodles up jellyroll fashion, starting at narrow end.

Pour spaghetti sauce into a lightly greased 13- x 9- x 2-inch baking dish. Cut lasagna rolls in half crosswise. Place rolls, cut side down, over sauce in dish. Sprinkle with remaining ½ cup Parmesan cheese.

Cover and bake at 350° for 25 minutes or until lasagna ruffles are thoroughly heated. Garnish, if desired. **Yield: 6 servings.**

Spinach-Stuffed Lasagna Ruffles Techniques

Place cooked lasagna noodles on layers of wax paper. Spread ½ cup spinach-cheese filling evenly over each noodle.

Carefully roll up each lasagna noodle lengthwise, keeping spinach-cheese mixture intact.

Cut each lasagna rollup in half crosswise. Place each half, cut side down, over sauce in dish.

Spinach-Stuffed Lasagna Ruffles

Southwestern Stuffed Shells

Southwestern Stuffed Shells

18 jumbo pasta shells, uncooked
1 (16-ounce) can pumpkin
1 large egg, lightly beaten
½ cup Italian-seasoned breadcrumbs
½ cup grated Parmesan cheese
½ teaspoon ground nutmeg
1 (16-ounce) jar picante sauce or salsa,
    divided
1 cup (4 ounces) shredded Monterey Jack
    cheese with peppers
2 tablespoons chopped fresh parsley
Garnish: fresh parsley sprigs

Cook pasta shells according to package directions; drain and set aside.

Combine pumpkin, egg, breadcrumbs, Parmesan cheese, and nutmeg; stuff each shell with mixture.

Spread 1 cup picante sauce in a lightly greased 13- x 9- x 2-inch baking dish. Place filled shells on sauce; top with remaining sauce.

Cover and bake at 350° for 35 minutes or until thoroughly heated. Arrange on individual plates, and sprinkle with Monterey Jack cheese and parsley. Garnish, if desired. **Yield: 3 to 4 servings.**

Satisfying Side Dishes

Mostaccioli Alfredo, Pesto Pasta, and Tortellini Carbonara
are just a sampling of the pasta side dishes that make
great family or entertaining fare.

Garlic Pasta with Marinara Sauce, Fettuccine with Poppy Seeds

Tortellini with Parsley-Caper Sauce, Tortellini Carbonara, St. Louis Toasted Ravioli

Toasted Rice and Pasta, Mostaccioli Alfredo, Lemon-Garlic Pasta, Pesto Pasta

Spinach Pesto-Pasta, Spinach Fettuccine with Mustard Greens

Macaroni and Cheese (page 103)

Garlic Pasta with Marinara Sauce

1 (9-ounce) package refrigerated angel hair
    pasta, uncooked
½ teaspoon salt
4 cloves garlic, minced
2 tablespoons olive oil
½ teaspoon freshly ground pepper
1 (15-ounce) carton refrigerated marinara
    sauce
Grated Parmesan cheese

Cook pasta according to package directions, adding ½ teaspoon salt; drain.

Cook minced garlic in oil in a small skillet over medium-high heat, stirring constantly; pour over pasta, and sprinkle with pepper, tossing gently.

Top pasta with marinara sauce, and sprinkle with cheese. **Yield: 3 servings.**

Toasted Rice and Pasta

1½ cups long-grain rice, uncooked
4 ounces angel hair pasta or vermicelli,
    uncooked and broken into 1½-inch pieces
2 tablespoons vegetable oil
1 large onion, chopped
2 (14½-ounce) cans ready-to-serve chicken
    broth
¼ cup chopped fresh parsley

Cook rice and pasta in oil in a Dutch oven over medium heat, stirring constantly, 3 to 5 minutes or until golden. Add onion, and cook mixture 3 minutes.

Stir in broth; bring to a boil. Cover, reduce heat to low, and simmer 15 to 17 minutes.

Stir in parsley, and serve immediately. **Yield: 4 to 6 servings.**

Fettuccine with Poppy Seeds

6 ounces fettuccine, uncooked
⅓ cup butter or margarine, melted
¾ teaspoon garlic salt
¾ teaspoon dried parsley flakes
½ teaspoon poppy seeds
⅛ teaspoon pepper
½ cup sour cream
½ cup grated Parmesan cheese

Cook fettuccine according to package directions; drain.

Combine butter and next 4 ingredients; stir in sour cream.

Combine fettuccine and sour cream mixture; add cheese, and toss until fettuccine is coated. Serve immediately. **Yield: 6 servings.**

Fresh Tomato Sauce over Basil Pasta

6 pounds tomatoes, peeled, seeded, and
    chopped (about 7 large)
16 cloves garlic, minced
1 teaspoon salt
½ teaspoon pepper
1 (16-ounce) package linguine, uncooked
¾ cup freshly grated Parmesan cheese
½ cup butter or margarine, softened
¼ cup chopped fresh basil or 1 tablespoon
    dried basil

Combine tomato and garlic in a heavy saucepan; bring to a boil. Reduce heat, and cook 15 to 20 minutes, stirring occasionally. Stir in salt and pepper; keep warm.

Cook linguine according to package directions; drain. Add Parmesan cheese, butter, and basil, tossing well. To serve, top pasta with tomato mixture. **Yield: 8 servings.**

Tri-Colored Fettuccine Alfredo

(pictured on page 2)

6 ounces fresh fettuccine, uncooked
5 ounces fresh spinach fettuccine, uncooked
5 ounces fresh tomato or sweet red pepper
    fettuccine, uncooked
¾ cup butter or margarine, melted
¼ teaspoon garlic powder
2 cups whipping cream
¼ cup grated Asiago cheese
¼ cup grated Romano cheese
¼ cup sour cream
¼ teaspoon salt
¼ cup grated Parmesan cheese
Freshly ground pepper to taste

   Cook fettuccine according to package directions; drain well. Place fettuccine in a large Dutch oven.

   Combine butter and garlic powder; pour over fettuccine. Gradually add whipping cream and next 4 ingredients; cook over low heat, stirring constantly, until mixture is thoroughly heated (do not boil).

   Transfer pasta mixture to a serving platter; sprinkle with Parmesan cheese and pepper to taste. Serve immediately. **Yield: 6 servings.**

Mostaccioli Alfredo

1 (16-ounce) package mostaccioli (tubular
    pasta), uncooked
1 cup whipping cream
½ cup butter or margarine
½ cup grated Parmesan cheese
¼ cup chopped fresh parsley
1 teaspoon salt
¼ teaspoon freshly ground pepper
⅛ teaspoon garlic powder

   Cook mostaccioli according to package directions; drain and set aside.

   Combine whipping cream and butter in a Dutch oven; heat until butter melts, stirring occasionally (do not boil).

   Add cheese and remaining 4 ingredients; stir well. Add mostaccioli, and toss well. Serve immediately. **Yield: 8 servings.**

Get Fresh with Pasta

Fresh pasta cooks more quickly than dried pasta because of its higher water content. Refrigerated pasta is squeezed from commercial pasta machines and then cut, cooled, and packaged; it does not go through drying machines as does dry pasta.

   Add fresh pasta to boiling, salted water; return to full boil, and start testing for doneness. Linguine and fettuccine may take no longer than 2 to 3 minutes, but use the package directions as a guide.

Fettuccine Alfredo

Fettuccine Alfredo

8 ounces fettuccine, uncooked
½ cup butter
½ cup whipping cream
¾ cup grated Parmesan cheese
¼ teaspoon ground white pepper
2 tablespoons chopped fresh parsley
Garnish: fresh parsley

Cook fettuccine according to package directions, omitting salt. Drain well, and place in a large bowl.

Combine butter and whipping cream in a small saucepan; cook over low heat until butter melts. Stir in cheese, pepper, and parsley.

Pour mixture over hot fettuccine; toss until fettuccine is coated. Garnish, if desired. **Yield: 4 servings.**

Lemon-Garlic Pasta

8 ounces thin spaghetti, uncooked
2 tablespoons butter or margarine
2 tablespoons olive oil
4 to 5 cloves garlic, minced
¼ cup lemon juice
¼ teaspoon salt
½ to 1 teaspoon pepper
⅓ cup chopped fresh parsley

Cook pasta according to package directions; drain and set aside.

Melt butter in a large skillet over medium-high heat; add olive oil and minced garlic. Cook, stirring constantly, 1 minute. Add lemon juice, salt, and pepper.

Bring mixture to a boil; pour over pasta. Add parsley; toss gently. Serve immediately. **Yield: 4 servings.**

Lemon Vermicelli

⅓ cup milk
3 tablespoons butter or margarine
1 (7-ounce) package vermicelli, uncooked
¼ cup lemon juice
⅓ cup grated Parmesan cheese
Garnishes: fresh parsley, lemon twists

Combine milk and butter in a saucepan; cook over low heat until butter melts. Set aside, and keep warm.

Cook vermicelli according to package directions; drain. Rinse with warm water; drain. Place in a bowl, and toss with lemon juice; let stand 1 minute.

Add cheese and warm milk mixture to pasta; toss well. Garnish, if desired. **Yield: 6 servings.**

Green Peas and Pasta

4 ounces spinach linguine, uncooked
1 cup whipping cream
1 cup chicken broth
½ cup freshly grated Parmesan cheese
½ cup frozen English peas
3 slices bacon, cooked and crumbled

Cook linguine according to package directions; drain and keep warm.

Combine whipping cream and chicken broth in a saucepan; bring to a boil. Reduce heat, and simmer 25 minutes or until thickened and reduced to 1 cup. Remove mixture from heat.

Add cheese, peas, and bacon, stirring until cheese melts. Toss with linguine, and serve immediately. **Yield: 2 servings.**

Note: Whipping cream and chicken broth may be simmered longer for a thicker sauce. Peeled, cooked shrimp or chopped, cooked chicken may be added with the cheese, peas, and bacon for a heartier dish.

Noodles Romanoff

Noodles Romanoff

1 (8-ounce) package medium-size curly egg
    noodles, uncooked
1 cup small-curd cottage cheese
1 (8-ounce) carton sour cream
½ cup sliced ripe olives
½ cup sliced green onions
1 teaspoon Worcestershire sauce
½ teaspoon salt
⅛ teaspoon ground red pepper
½ cup (2 ounces) shredded Cheddar cheese

Cook noodles according to package directions,
omitting salt. Drain well.

Combine noodles, cottage cheese, and next 6
ingredients, stirring well. Spoon mixture into a
lightly greased 11- x 7- x 1½-inch baking dish.

Bake, uncovered, at 350° for 30 minutes.
Sprinkle with shredded Cheddar cheese, and bake
5 additional minutes or until cheese melts. **Yield:
6 to 8 servings.**

Traditional Pesto and Linguine

½ cup packed chopped fresh basil
¼ cup chopped fresh parsley
¼ cup grated Parmesan cheese
2 tablespoons pine nuts or walnuts
1 clove garlic, halved
2 tablespoons olive oil
2 tablespoons butter or margarine, softened
¼ teaspoon salt
¼ teaspoon pepper
6 ounces linguine, uncooked

Combine first 9 ingredients in container of an
electric blender. Cover and process at high until
smooth.

Cook linguine according to package directions;
drain. Spoon pesto mixture over linguine. Toss
gently; serve immediately. **Yield: 3 to 4 servings.**

Spinach Pesto-Pasta

1 (10-ounce) package frozen chopped spinach,
    thawed
½ cup grated Parmesan cheese
⅓ cup fresh basil leaves
¼ cup pine nuts, toasted
1 teaspoon crushed garlic
½ teaspoon coarsely ground pepper
¼ teaspoon anise seed, ground
¼ teaspoon salt
2 tablespoons butter or margarine, softened
½ cup olive oil
1 (12-ounce) package egg noodles, uncooked

Drain spinach on paper towels.

Combine spinach and next 9 ingredients in a
food processor bowl fitted with knife blade.
Process 30 seconds, stopping once to scrape
down sides.

Cook noodles according to package directions;
drain well. Add pesto to hot noodles, tossing gently. Serve immediately. **Yield: 8 to 10 servings.**

Make Fresh Pesto

Pesto, a fresh-tasting sauce that adds
flavor and color to pasta, originated
in Italy. The first pesto was made with
a mortar and pestle, but today you
can whip up the uncooked sauce in
an electric blender or food processor.

Pesto is usually made with fresh
basil, garlic, pine nuts, Parmesan
cheese, and olive oil. Make pesto in
large batches, and freeze in ice cube
trays. When frozen, put pesto cubes
in a freezer bag, and freeze up to 6
months.

Pesto Pasta

5 ounces fresh spinach
1 cup fresh parsley sprigs
⅔ cup grated Parmesan cheese
½ cup chopped walnuts, toasted
6 cloves garlic, split
4 anchovy fillets
3 tablespoons minced fresh tarragon or
    1 tablespoon dried tarragon
1 tablespoon minced fresh basil or 1 teaspoon
    dried basil
½ teaspoon salt
½ teaspoon pepper
¾ cup olive oil
1 (16-ounce) package thin spaghetti, uncooked
Garnish: fresh basil leaves

Remove stems from spinach. Wash leaves thoroughly in lukewarm water; drain and pat dry.

Position knife blade in food processor bowl; add spinach. Process until spinach is finely chopped.

Add parsley and next 8 ingredients; process until smooth. With processor running, pour oil through food chute in a slow, steady stream until combined.

Cook pasta according to package directions; drain well. Place in a large serving bowl. Toss pasta with pesto. Garnish, if desired. **Yield: 8 to 10 servings.**

Pesto Pasta Techniques

Always wash fresh spinach leaves, and remove tough stems. Drain spinach, and pat dry with paper towels.

Anchovies, a saltwater fish with oily flesh, contribute a pleasing flavor to pesto.

Add olive oil to spinach mixture in a slow, steady stream. It will blend quickly to make a thick pesto.

Pesto Pasta

Spinach Fettuccine with Mustard Greens

1½ pounds fresh mustard greens
10 ounces spinach fettuccine, uncooked
1 cup whipping cream
4 ounces goat cheese
¼ teaspoon salt
½ teaspoon freshly ground pepper
2 tablespoons butter or margarine
2 cloves garlic, minced
¼ cup water
½ cup coarsely chopped walnuts, toasted

Remove and discard stems and any discolored spots from greens. Wash greens thoroughly; drain. Cut into 1-inch strips; set aside.

Cook fettuccine according to package directions; drain and set aside.

Bring whipping cream to a boil in a heavy saucepan; boil until cream is reduced to ¾ cup. Remove from heat; add goat cheese, salt, and pepper, stirring with a spoon or wire whisk until smooth. Set aside.

Melt butter in a large heavy skillet over medium heat; add garlic, and cook 1 minute. Gradually add greens, stirring after each addition until leaves wilt. Add water; cover and cook 10 minutes or until tender, stirring occasionally. Drain.

Return greens to skillet; add cream mixture. Cook over medium heat, stirring constantly, 1 minute or until thoroughly heated.

Combine greens mixture, fettuccine, and walnuts; toss gently. Serve pasta immediately. **Yield: 6 to 8 side-dish servings or 3 to 4 main-dish servings.**

Note: Regular spaghetti noodles may be substituted for spinach fettuccine.

Vermicelli with Fresh Spinach Sauce

1 (8-ounce) package vermicelli, uncooked
2 tablespoons butter or margarine
½ pound fresh chopped spinach
½ teaspoon salt
½ teaspoon pepper
1 cup part-skim ricotta cheese
¼ cup milk
½ cup grated fresh Parmesan cheese

Cook vermicelli according to package directions; drain and set aside.

Melt butter in a large skillet. Add spinach; cook over medium heat, stirring constantly, 10 minutes.

Add salt and next 3 ingredients to spinach; cook over low heat, stirring constantly, until mixture is heated (do not boil).

Add grated Parmesan cheese, tossing well. Serve over hot vermicelli. **Yield: 4 servings.**

Glorious Macaroni

1 (8-ounce) package shell macaroni, uncooked
¼ cup chopped onion
1 (2-ounce) jar diced pimiento, drained
1 tablespoon butter or margarine, melted
2 cups (8 ounces) shredded Cheddar cheese
1 (10¾-ounce) can cream of mushroom soup, undiluted
½ cup mayonnaise
1 (2½-ounce) jar sliced mushrooms, drained

Cook macaroni in a Dutch oven according to package directions; drain.

Cook onion and pimiento in butter until onion is crisp-tender.

Combine macaroni, onion mixture, cheese, and remaining ingredients; mix well. Spoon into a lightly greased 2-quart shallow baking dish.

Bake at 350° for 30 minutes. **Yield: 6 servings.**

Old-Fashioned Macaroni and Cheese

1 (8-ounce) package elbow macaroni, uncooked
2½ cups (10 ounces) shredded Cheddar cheese, divided
2 large eggs, lightly beaten
1½ cups milk
1 teaspoon salt
⅛ teaspoon ground white pepper
Paprika

Cook macaroni according to package directions; drain.

Layer one-third each of macaroni and cheese in a lightly greased 2-quart baking dish. Repeat procedure, and top with remaining macaroni. (Reserve remaining cheese.)

Combine eggs, milk, salt, and pepper; pour over macaroni and cheese.

Cover and bake at 350° for 45 minutes. Uncover and sprinkle with remaining cheese and paprika.

Cover and let stand 10 minutes before serving.
Yield: 6 to 8 servings.

Macaroni and Cheese

(pictured on page 93)

1 (8-ounce) package elbow macaroni, uncooked
¼ cup butter or margarine
¼ cup plus 2 tablespoons all-purpose flour
¼ teaspoon salt
2 cups milk
2 cups (8 ounces) shredded Cheddar cheese
1 (2-ounce) jar diced pimiento, drained
1 tablespoon butter or margarine
⅓ cup fine, dry breadcrumbs
½ teaspoon dried parsley flakes

Cook macaroni according to package directions; drain and set aside.

Place ¼ cup butter in a 4-cup glass measure; microwave, uncovered, at HIGH 55 seconds or until melted.

Blend in flour and salt, stirring until smooth. Gradually stir in milk; microwave, uncovered, at HIGH 5 to 6 minutes or until thickened, stirring after every minute. Add cheese, stirring until melted; stir in pimiento.

Add cheese sauce to macaroni, stirring well. Place macaroni mixture in a 1½-quart baking dish. Cover with heavy-duty plastic wrap; fold back a small edge of wrap to allow steam to escape.

Microwave at MEDIUM HIGH (70% power) 7 to 8 minutes or until thoroughly heated, stirring after 4 minutes.

Place 1 tablespoon butter in a 1-cup glass measure; microwave, uncovered, at HIGH 35 seconds or until melted. Stir in breadcrumbs and parsley flakes; sprinkle over macaroni mixture. Let stand, uncovered, 1 minute. Serve immediately. **Yield: 6 servings.**

From top: Macaroni and Blue Cheese, Jack-in-the-Macaroni Bake, Creamy Macaroni and Cheese

Creamy Macaroni and Cheese

1 (8-ounce) package elbow macaroni,
    uncooked
4 cups (16 ounces) shredded Cheddar or
    Jarlsberg cheese
1 (8-ounce) carton sour cream
1 cup mayonnaise
2 tablespoons chopped onion
1 cup cheese crackers, crushed
Garnish: green onion fan

    Cook macaroni according to package directions; drain. Rinse with cold water; drain.
    Combine macaroni and next 4 ingredients. Spoon into a lightly greased 11- x 7- x 1½-inch baking dish; sprinkle with crushed crackers.
    Bake at 325° for 30 to 35 minutes. Garnish, if desired. **Yield: 6 to 8 servings.**

Jack-in-the-Macaroni Bake

1 (8-ounce) package elbow macaroni,
    uncooked
2 tablespoons butter or margarine
¼ cup chopped onion
¼ cup chopped sweet red pepper
2 cups (8 ounces) shredded Monterey Jack
    cheese with peppers
1 (10¾-ounce) can cream of celery soup,
    undiluted
½ cup sour cream
Chili powder
Garnish: celery leaves

    Cook macaroni according to package directions; drain. Rinse with cold water; drain.
    Melt butter in a Dutch oven; add onion and sweet red pepper. Cook over medium heat, stirring constantly, until vegetables are crisp-tender. Remove from heat.

    Stir cheese, soup, and sour cream into Dutch oven. Stir in macaroni; spoon into a lightly greased 2-quart shallow baking dish. Sprinkle with chili powder.
    Bake at 350° for 30 minutes. Garnish, if desired. **Yield: 6 servings.**

Macaroni and Blue Cheese

1 (8-ounce) package elbow macaroni,
    uncooked
¼ cup butter or margarine
¼ cup all-purpose flour
2 cups milk
1 (4-ounce) package crumbled blue cheese
1 large egg, lightly beaten
1 (2-ounce) jar diced pimiento, drained
½ cup soft breadcrumbs
½ cup walnuts, finely chopped
Garnish: fresh parsley sprig

    Cook macaroni according to package directions; drain. Rinse with cold water; drain.
    Melt butter in a Dutch oven over low heat; add flour, stirring until mixture is smooth. Cook, stirring constantly, 1 minute. Gradually add milk; cook over medium heat, stirring constantly, until mixture is thickened.
    Add blue cheese, stirring until melted. Stir about one-fourth of hot cheese mixture into egg; add to remaining hot mixture, stirring constantly.
    Stir in macaroni and pimiento; spoon into a lightly greased 2-quart shallow baking dish. Sprinkle with breadcrumbs and walnuts.
    Bake at 350° for 35 minutes. Garnish, if desired. **Yield: 6 servings.**

Mushroom-Macaroni Casserole

1 (8-ounce) package elbow macaroni,
    uncooked
1 (10¾-ounce) can cream of mushroom soup,
    undiluted
1 cup mayonnaise
2 cups (8 ounces) shredded sharp Cheddar
    cheese
1 (4-ounce) can sliced mushrooms, drained
1 (2-ounce) jar diced pimiento, drained
    (optional)
¾ cup crushed round buttery crackers (about
    15 crackers)
1 tablespoon butter or margarine, melted

Cook macaroni according to package directions; drain. Rinse with cold water; drain.

Combine macaroni, soup, and next 3 ingredients; add pimiento, if desired. Spoon into a lightly greased 2-quart baking dish.

Combine cracker crumbs and melted butter; sprinkle evenly over macaroni mixture.

Bake at 300° for 30 minutes or until thoroughly heated. **Yield: 6 to 8 servings.**

Orzo and Olive Bake

½ (16-ounce) package orzo (rice-shaped
    pasta), uncooked
1 large onion, chopped
1 cup chopped celery
2 tablespoons olive oil
1 tablespoon all-purpose flour
1 (16-ounce) can Italian-style tomatoes,
    drained
½ cup canned diluted chicken broth
1 teaspoon dried oregano
1 (4-ounce) can sliced ripe olives, drained
2 cups (8 ounces) shredded mozzarella cheese,
    divided
¾ teaspoon salt
¼ teaspoon ground red pepper

Cook orzo according to package directions; drain and set aside.

Cook onion and celery in oil in a large skillet over medium heat, stirring constantly, until tender. Add flour, stirring constantly until blended.

Add tomatoes, broth, and oregano; simmer 5 minutes. Stir in orzo, olives, 1 cup cheese, and salt. Spoon mixture into a greased 1½-quart baking dish. Sprinkle with remaining cheese and pepper.

Bake, uncovered, at 400° for 20 minutes. **Yield: 6 servings.**

Orzo and Olive Bake Technique

Stir orzo into simmering tomato mixture.

Orzo and Olive Bake

St. Louis Toasted Ravioli

1 large egg, lightly beaten
2 tablespoons milk
¾ cup dry Italian-seasoned breadcrumbs
½ teaspoon salt (optional)
½ (27.5-ounce) package frozen cheese-filled
    ravioli, thawed
Vegetable oil
Grated Parmesan cheese
Commercial spaghetti sauce or pizza sauce

Combine egg and milk in a small bowl. Place breadcrumbs and, if desired, salt, in a shallow bowl. Dip ravioli in milk mixture, and coat with breadcrumbs.

Pour oil to a depth of 2 inches into a Dutch oven; heat to 350°.

Fry ravioli, a few at a time, 1 minute on each side or until golden. Drain on paper towels.

Sprinkle with Parmesan cheese, and serve immediately with warm spaghetti sauce or pizza sauce. **Yield: about 2 dozen appetizers or 4 to 6 side-dish servings.**

Note: Refrigerated fresh ravioli may be substituted for the frozen. Vary the flavor by using sausage, chicken, Italian, or other meat-filled varieties.

Ravioli with Creamy Pesto Sauce
(pictured on page 45)

2 (9-ounce) packages refrigerated cheese-filled
    ravioli, uncooked
1 cup whipping cream
1 (2.82-ounce) jar pesto sauce
1 (3-ounce) jar capers, drained (optional)
2 tablespoons pine nuts, toasted

Cook pasta according to package directions; drain well.

Combine whipping cream and pesto sauce in a saucepan; add capers, if desired. Cook over low

heat until thoroughly heated, stirring frequently.

Toss ravioli with sauce, and sprinkle with toasted pine nuts. Serve immediately. **Yield: 6 servings.**

Spinach Tortellini with Tomato Sauce

1 (9-ounce) package refrigerated spinach
    tortellini, uncooked
2 cloves garlic, minced
2 tablespoons chopped onion
2 tablespoons olive oil
½ green pepper, chopped
1 hot pepper, seeded and chopped
2 large tomatoes, peeled and chopped
½ teaspoon dried oregano
½ teaspoon dried basil
½ cup freshly grated Parmesan cheese

Cook tortellini according to package directions; drain. Spoon onto platter.

Cook garlic and onion in olive oil, stirring constantly, 3 minutes or until crisp-tender. Add peppers, and cook 1 minute.

Add tomato, oregano, and basil; cook, stirring constantly, 3 minutes.

Spoon mixture over tortellini, and sprinkle with cheese. Serve immediately. **Yield: 3 to 4 servings.**

Spinach Tortellini with Tomato Sauce

Tortellini Carbonara

Tortellini with Parsley-Caper Sauce

1 to 2 cloves garlic
¾ cup finely chopped fresh parsley
¼ cup grated Parmesan cheese
2 tablespoons sunflower kernels
2 tablespoons capers
⅛ teaspoon salt
⅛ teaspoon pepper
½ cup olive oil
1 (9-ounce) package refrigerated cheese-filled
     tortellini, uncooked
1½ teaspoons olive oil

Position knife blade in food processor bowl. Drop garlic through food chute with processor running; process 5 seconds or until minced.

Add parsley and next 5 ingredients; process until smooth, stopping occasionally to scrape down sides. Gradually pour ½ cup olive oil through food chute with processor running, blending just until mixture is smooth. Set aside.

Cook tortellini according to package directions; drain. Add 1½ teaspoons olive oil; toss gently.

Pour sauce over tortellini, and toss. **Yield: 25 appetizer servings or 3 to 4 side-dish servings.**

Tortellini Carbonara

1 (9-ounce) package refrigerated cheese-filled
     tortellini, uncooked
1 small clove garlic, minced
1½ teaspoons olive oil
½ teaspoon white vinegar
3 slices bacon, cooked and crumbled
⅓ cup grated Parmesan cheese
¼ cup whipping cream
1 tablespoon minced fresh parsley
¼ teaspoon pepper

Cook tortellini according to package directions; drain. Cook garlic in hot oil in a small saucepan over medium-high heat; stir in vinegar.

Add garlic mixture, bacon, and remaining ingredients to tortellini; toss gently to combine. Serve immediately. **Yield: 3 to 4 servings.**

Keep Parsley Fresh

Extend the life of fresh parsley by placing it in a glass jar with a small amount of water. Cover the jar tightly, and refrigerate, changing the water at least every 5 days.

Salad Sampler

Let pasta salad star at your next picnic or casual supper. You'll find the marriage of cold pasta and poultry, meats, or vegetables to be a satisfying match.

Cold Pasta Platter, Chicken-and-Broccoli Pasta, Primavera Salad

Artichokes with Orzo Salad, Bow Tie Pasta Primavera, Garden Tortellini Salad

Smoked Turkey Pasta Primavera, Ham and Cheese Salad, Black-Eyed Pea Salad

Pasta Antipasto, Crabmeat-Shrimp Pasta Salad, Antipasto Kabobs

Cheddar-Pasta Toss (page 115)

Cold Pasta Platter

Place chicken in a Dutch oven; add water to cover. Bring to a boil; cover, reduce heat, and simmer 45 minutes or until chicken is tender.

Remove chicken from broth, and cool. Bone chicken, and cut into ½-inch pieces; set aside.

Combine vinegar and next 4 ingredients, mixing well. Gradually add olive oil and vegetable oil; whisk until blended. Set dressing aside.

Cook vermicelli according to package directions, omitting salt; drain. Rinse with cold water; drain well.

Combine pasta and dressing, tossing well. Add chicken and mayonnaise, mixing well; cover and chill at least 1 hour.

Spoon mixture into center of a lettuce-lined platter. Sprinkle with chopped parsley, if desired. Arrange beets, mushrooms, artichoke hearts, and tomatoes around pasta. Garnish, if desired. **Yield: about 6 servings.**

Cold Pasta Platter

1 (3-pound) broiler-fryer
¼ cup white wine vinegar
2 teaspoons Dijon mustard
2 teaspoons chopped garlic
½ teaspoon salt
½ teaspoon freshly ground pepper
2 tablespoons olive oil
2 tablespoons vegetable oil
8 ounces vermicelli, uncooked
½ cup mayonnaise
Leaf lettuce
2 tablespoons chopped fresh parsley
    (optional)
Pickled beets
Marinated mushrooms
Marinated artichoke hearts
Cherry tomatoes
Garnish: parsley sprigs

Chicken-and-Broccoli Pasta

4 skinned chicken breast halves
3 cups broccoli flowerets
8 ounces rotini (corkscrew pasta), uncooked
½ cup chopped walnuts, toasted
½ cup grated fresh Parmesan cheese
1 tablespoon lemon juice
1 teaspoon dried basil
¾ cup mayonnaise

Place chicken in a Dutch oven; add water to cover. Bring to a boil; cover, reduce heat, and simmer 20 to 25 minutes or until chicken is tender.

Remove chicken from broth, and cool. Bone chicken, and chop. Cover and chill.

Place broccoli in a steaming rack; place over boiling water. Cover and steam 7 minutes or until crisp-tender. Let cool.

Cook pasta according to package directions, omitting salt; drain. Rinse with cold water; drain.

Place chicken, broccoli, and pasta in a large bowl; add walnuts and remaining ingredients, and toss gently. Cover and chill. **Yield: 4 to 6 servings.**

Tarragon Pasta-Chicken Salad

1 (8-ounce) bottle Italian salad dressing
¼ cup white wine vinegar
2 tablespoons chopped fresh tarragon
1 clove garlic, minced
4 skinned and boned chicken breast halves
4 ounces shell macaroni, uncooked
2 cups sliced celery
½ cup chopped sweet red pepper or green pepper
¼ cup chopped green onions
1 tablespoon chopped fresh parsley
½ cup mayonnaise

Combine first 4 ingredients in a jar, and cover tightly. Shake vigorously until well mixed.

Place chicken in a heavy-duty, zip-top plastic bag; pour ¾ cup dressing mixture over chicken, reserving remaining mixture. Seal bag, and chill at least 8 hours.

Transfer chicken and marinade from bag to an 11- x 7- x 1½-inch baking dish. Bake at 350° for 25 to 30 minutes or until done. Drain chicken, and cool slightly; coarsely chop.

Cook pasta according to package directions; drain and cool slightly.

Combine chicken, reserved dressing mixture, pasta, celery, and remaining ingredients in a large bowl; toss gently. Cover and chill thoroughly. **Yield: 4 to 6 servings.**

Fruited Pasta Salad

1⅓ cups rotini (corkscrew pasta), uncooked
2 cups chopped cooked chicken
1½ cups sliced celery
1 cup seedless green grapes, halved
¼ cup chopped green pepper
¼ cup chopped purple onion
1 (11-ounce) can mandarin oranges, drained
1 (8-ounce) can sliced water chestnuts, drained
¼ cup commercial buttermilk dressing
¼ cup mayonnaise
1 teaspoon Beau Monde seasoning
¼ teaspoon salt
⅛ teaspoon pepper

Cook pasta according to package directions; drain. Rinse with cold water; drain.

Combine pasta and next 7 ingredients in a large bowl, tossing gently.

Combine buttermilk dressing and next 4 ingredients. Pour over pasta mixture, tossing gently. Cover and chill. **Yield: 4 to 6 servings.**

Pasta Technique

Draining and rinsing hot cooked pasta in cold water helps to cool it quickly before tossing it with other ingredients.

Smoked Turkey Pasta Primavera

1 (12-ounce) package fettuccine, uncooked
1½ pounds fresh broccoli, cut into flowerets
2 medium zucchini, thinly sliced
6 green onions, thinly sliced
1 sweet red pepper, sliced into thin strips
1 (6-ounce) can pitted ripe olives, drained and
    sliced
4 cups chopped cooked smoked turkey
⅔ cup grated Parmesan cheese
½ teaspoon salt
½ teaspoon freshly ground pepper
Basil Sauce
2 cups cherry tomatoes, halved
Lettuce leaves

Cook fettuccine according to package directions; drain. Rinse with cold water; drain.

Combine fettuccine and next 9 ingredients. Add Basil Sauce and cherry tomatoes; toss gently.

Cover and chill. Serve on lettuce leaves.
Yield: 12 servings.

Basil Sauce

⅓ cup chopped fresh basil
1 clove garlic
¼ teaspoon dry mustard
¼ teaspoon salt
¼ teaspoon lemon juice
2 teaspoons white wine vinegar
⅓ cup mayonnaise
⅓ cup sour cream

Combine basil and garlic in container of an electric blender or food processor; process 30 seconds or until basil is finely chopped.

Add mustard and next 3 ingredients; process 20 seconds, stopping once to scrape down sides.

Add mayonnaise and sour cream. Stir well.
Yield: ⅔ cup.

Primavera Salad

Primavera Salad

1 pound broccoli
1 (12-ounce) package bow tie pasta, uncooked
Versatile Vinaigrette
1 (10-ounce) package fresh spinach
1 pound smoked turkey breast, cut into thin
    strips
1 pint cherry tomatoes, halved
½ cup chopped fresh basil
¼ cup chopped fresh parsley
⅓ cup pine nuts, toasted

Remove broccoli leaves, and cut off tough ends of stalks; discard. Wash broccoli thoroughly, and cut into 1-inch pieces.

Cook broccoli in boiling water to cover 1 minute; drain immediately, and plunge into ice water. Drain and pat dry with paper towels; chill.

Cook pasta according to package directions; drain. Rinse with cold water; drain.

Combine pasta and Versatile Vinaigrette, tossing to coat. Place in a large heavy-duty, zip-top plastic bag. Chill at least 2 hours or overnight.

Remove stems from spinach; wash leaves thoroughly, and pat dry.

Combine spinach, broccoli, pasta, turkey, and remaining ingredients, tossing gently. **Yield: 8 to 10 servings.**

Versatile Vinaigrette

⅔ cup vegetable oil
¼ cup white wine vinegar
¼ cup water
1½ teaspoons salt
1 tablespoon freshly ground pepper
1 clove garlic, crushed

Combine all ingredients in a jar. Cover tightly, and shake vigorously. **Yield: 1 cup.**

Ranch-Style Turkey 'n' Pasta Salad

2 cups penne (short tubular pasta), uncooked
2 cups chopped cooked turkey
1 small zucchini, sliced
2 small yellow squash, sliced
1 small green pepper, seeded and chopped
1 small sweet red pepper, seeded and chopped
¼ cup grated Parmesan cheese
¾ cup commercial Ranch-style dressing

Cook pasta according to package directions; drain. Rinse with cold water; drain.

Combine pasta and remaining ingredients in a large bowl. Cover and chill at least 2 hours. Toss before serving. **Yield: 6 to 8 servings.**

Cheddar-Pasta Toss

(pictured on page 111)

1½ cups tri-colored rotini (corkscrew pasta), uncooked
½ (10-ounce) package frozen English peas
1 cup julienne-sliced cooked ham
1 (8-ounce) package Cheddar cheese, cut into ¾-inch cubes
½ cup chopped celery
½ cup sliced ripe olives
3 green onions, chopped
⅓ cup mayonnaise
2 tablespoons red wine vinegar
1 tablespoon olive oil
¼ teaspoon garlic powder
¼ teaspoon pepper
⅛ teaspoon dried oregano
1 (4-ounce) jar diced pimiento, drained
Lettuce leaves

Cook rotini according to package directions; drain. Rinse with cold water; drain.

Cook peas according to package directions; drain well. Combine pasta, peas, ham, and next 4 ingredients in a large bowl; toss gently.

Combine mayonnaise and next 5 ingredients in a small bowl; stir well. Add to pasta mixture; toss gently to coat.

Cover and chill thoroughly. Stir in pimiento just before serving. Serve salad on lettuce leaves. **Yield: 6 servings.**

Ham and Cheese Salad

Ham and Cheese Salad

8 ounces rotini (corkscrew pasta), uncooked
½ pound cooked ham, cut into 2-inch strips
1 cup broccoli flowerets
1 cup frozen English peas, thawed
1 small yellow squash, thinly sliced
1 small sweet red pepper, cut into thin strips
4 ounces Swiss cheese, cubed
½ cup mayonnaise
¼ cup Dijon mustard
¼ cup milk
¼ cup grated Parmesan cheese

Cook pasta according to package directions; drain. Rinse with cold water; drain.

Combine pasta and next 6 ingredients in a large bowl.

Combine mayonnaise, mustard, and milk; stir well. Add to vegetable mixture, tossing gently. Sprinkle with Parmesan cheese. Cover and chill at least 2 hours. **Yield: 6 servings.**

Italian Salad

1 (12-ounce) package rotini (corkscrew pasta), uncooked
2 (6-ounce) jars marinated artichoke hearts, undrained
1¼ cups pitted ripe olives, sliced
1 cup chopped green pepper
¼ pound hard salami, cut into ¼-inch strips
½ cup grated Parmesan cheese
¼ cup chopped onion
¼ cup chopped fresh parsley
1 (0.7-ounce) package Italian salad dressing mix

Cook pasta according to package directions; drain. Rinse with cold water; drain.

Drain artichokes, reserving ¼ cup liquid; set aside. Cut artichoke hearts into quarters; set aside.

Combine pasta, artichokes, reserved artichoke liquid, olives, and remaining ingredients in a large bowl; toss gently. Cover and chill. **Yield: 6 servings.**

Pasta Antipasto

1 cup rotini (corkscrew pasta), uncooked
2 (6-ounce) jars marinated artichoke hearts, undrained
¾ cup commercial Italian salad dressing
¼ teaspoon freshly ground pepper
1 pint cherry tomatoes
½ cup pimiento-stuffed olives
½ cup ripe olives
2 medium carrots, scraped and cut into very thin strips
½ pound fresh mushrooms
1 medium-size green pepper, cut into strips
3 to 4 ounces sliced pepperoni
3 to 4 ounces sliced salami

Cook pasta according to package directions, omitting salt; drain. Rinse with cold water; drain. Set aside.

Drain artichoke hearts, reserving ½ cup artichoke liquid. Add Italian salad dressing and ground pepper to reserved artichoke liquid to make marinade, stirring well.

Combine artichoke hearts, tomatoes, and next 5 ingredients. Add about three-fourths of marinade to vegetable mixture, tossing gently. Cover and chill 8 hours. Add remaining marinade to pasta, tossing gently. Cover and chill 8 hours.

Arrange pepperoni and salami around outer edges of a serving platter. Spoon pasta in a ring within meat, using a slotted spoon. Spoon vegetable mixture in center of platter, using a slotted spoon. **Yield: 8 to 10 servings.**

Pasta Salad

4 ounces spaghetti, uncooked
1 (6-ounce) jar marinated artichoke hearts, undrained
¾ cup sliced fresh zucchini
⅔ cup shredded carrot
2 ounces sliced salami, cut into strips
1 cup (4 ounces) shredded mozzarella cheese
2 tablespoons grated Parmesan cheese
2 tablespoons vegetable oil
2 tablespoons white wine vinegar
¾ teaspoon dry mustard
½ teaspoon dried oregano
½ teaspoon dried basil
1 clove garlic, crushed

Break spaghetti in half, and cook according to package directions, omitting salt; drain. Rinse with cold water; drain.

Drain artichoke hearts, reserving liquid; chop artichokes.

Combine spaghetti, artichokes, and next 5 ingredients; set aside.

Combine reserved artichoke liquid, oil, and next 5 ingredients in a jar. Cover tightly; shake.

Pour dressing over spaghetti mixture; toss gently to coat. Cover and chill 2 to 3 hours. **Yield: 6 to 8 servings.**

Salad Dressing Technique

Remove artichokes from liquid, and chop; use reserved liquid in the salad dressing.

Black-Eyed Pea Salad

1 (16-ounce) package dried black-eyed peas
6 cups water
1 (6-ounce) jar marinated artichoke hearts, undrained
2 cups cooked wagon wheel pasta
1 medium-size sweet red pepper, seeded and chopped
1 medium-size green pepper, seeded and chopped
¾ cup canned garbanzo beans
½ cup chopped purple onion
1 (6-ounce) package sliced provolone cheese, cut into strips
1 (3½-ounce) package sliced pepperoni, cut into strips
3 tablespoons chopped fresh parsley
1 (0.7-ounce) envelope Italian salad dressing mix
¼ cup sugar
½ teaspoon pepper
½ cup white wine vinegar
¼ cup vegetable oil

Sort and wash peas; place in a large Dutch oven. Cover with water 2 inches above peas; let soak 8 hours. Drain. Add 6 cups water, and bring to a boil. Cover, reduce heat, and simmer 45 minutes or until peas are tender. Drain and let cool.

Drain artichoke hearts, reserving liquid. Chop artichokes, and set aside.

Combine peas, chopped artichoke, pasta, and next 7 ingredients in a large bowl. Toss gently.

Combine reserved artichoke liquid, salad dressing mix, and next 4 ingredients in a jar; cover tightly, and shake vigorously.

Pour dressing over pea mixture, stirring gently. Cover and chill salad at least 2 hours before serving. **Yield: 12 servings.**

Black-Eyed Pea Salad

Crabmeat-Shrimp Pasta Salad

3 cups water
1 pound unpeeled medium-size fresh shrimp
6 ounces shell macaroni, uncooked
1 cup thinly sliced celery
½ medium-size green pepper, finely chopped
½ medium-size sweet red pepper, finely chopped
½ small purple onion, chopped
2 green onions, chopped
1 tablespoon chopped fresh parsley
¼ cup mayonnaise
¼ cup commercial Italian salad dressing
1 tablespoon lemon juice
½ teaspoon dried oregano, crushed
¼ teaspoon salt
Dash of pepper
8 ounces lump crabmeat, drained

Bring water to a boil; add shrimp, and cook 3 to 5 minutes or just until shrimp turn pink. Drain well; rinse shrimp with cold water. Chill. Peel shrimp, and devein, if desired; set aside.

Cook pasta according to package directions, omitting salt; drain. Rinse with cold water; drain. Stir in celery and next 5 ingredients.

Combine mayonnaise and next 5 ingredients; add to pasta mixture. Stir in crabmeat and shrimp. Cover and chill. **Yield: 7 servings.**

Salad Tip

Cold pasta has a tendency to stick together if it's not rinsed after cooking. For this reason, most of the salad recipes suggest rinsing cooked pasta with cold water before proceeding with the recipe.

Shrimp Vermicelli Salad

5 cups water
1½ pounds unpeeled medium-size fresh shrimp
1 (12-ounce) package vermicelli, uncooked
3 hard-cooked eggs, chopped
1½ cups chopped green onions
1 cup chopped dill pickle
¼ cup minced fresh parsley
1 small green pepper, seeded and chopped
1 (2-ounce) jar diced pimiento, drained
1 (10-ounce) package frozen tiny English peas, thawed and drained
1 cup mayonnaise
1 (8-ounce) carton sour cream
¼ cup lemon juice
2 tablespoons prepared mustard
1 teaspoon celery seeds
1 teaspoon salt
¼ teaspoon pepper
Leaf lettuce
¼ to ½ teaspoon paprika

Bring water to a boil; add shrimp, and cook 3 to 5 minutes or just until shrimp turn pink. Drain well; rinse with cold water. Chill. Peel shrimp, and devein, if desired.

Break vermicelli into 3-inch pieces. Cook according to package directions; drain. Rinse with cold water; drain.

Add shrimp, eggs, and next 6 ingredients to pasta; set aside.

Combine mayonnaise and next 6 ingredients; stir well. Pour over shrimp mixture; toss gently. Cover and chill 2 hours.

Serve on a lettuce-lined platter; sprinkle with paprika. **Yield: 8 servings.**

Shrimp-Pasta Medley

Shrimp-Pasta Medley

5 cups water

1½ pounds unpeeled medium-size fresh shrimp

1 cup rotini (corkscrew pasta), uncooked

1 (6-ounce) package frozen snow pea pods, thawed

1 (4-ounce) can button mushrooms, drained

⅓ to ½ cup grated Parmesan cheese

¼ cup sliced celery

¼ cup sliced pimiento-stuffed olives

¼ cup sliced ripe olives

1 teaspoon chopped parsley

1 teaspoon white wine

¼ teaspoon anise flavoring

1 (8-ounce) bottle Italian salad dressing

Lettuce leaves

Parmesan cheese

Garnish: cherry tomato halves

Bring water to a boil; add shrimp, and cook 3 to 5 minutes or just until shrimp turn pink. Drain well, and rinse with cold water. Chill. Peel shrimp, and devein, if desired.

Cook pasta according to package directions, omitting salt; drain. Rinse with cold water; drain.

Combine pasta, shrimp, snow peas, and next 9 ingredients, tossing well; chill at least 1 hour.

Spoon mixture onto a lettuce-lined platter. Sprinkle with Parmesan cheese. Garnish, if desired. **Yield: 6 servings.**

Bow Tie Shrimp Salad

Bow Tie Shrimp Salad

10 ounces bow tie pasta, uncooked
2 cups water
¾ pound unpeeled medium-size fresh shrimp
1½ cups frozen tiny English peas, thawed
1 (7-ounce) jar sun-dried tomatoes in oil,
    drained and coarsely chopped
1 small purple onion, finely chopped
½ cup finely chopped green pepper
½ cup finely chopped sweet yellow pepper
5 radishes, chopped
2 tablespoons minced fresh parsley
1 tablespoon minced fresh basil
3 tablespoons olive oil
2 tablespoons lemon juice
2 tablespoons white wine vinegar
1 teaspoon Dijon mustard
¼ teaspoon salt
Freshly ground pepper to taste

Cook pasta according to package directions; drain. Rinse with cold water; drain. Set aside.

Bring 2 cups water to a boil; add shrimp, and cook 3 to 5 minutes or just until shrimp turn pink. Drain; rinse with cold water. Chill. Peel shrimp, and devein, if desired.

Combine pasta, shrimp, peas, and next 7 ingredients in a large salad bowl. Toss gently, and set aside.

Combine olive oil and next 5 ingredients in a jar. Cover tightly; shake vigorously. Pour dressing over pasta mixture; toss gently. **Yield: 8 to 10 servings.**

Bow Tie Shrimp Salad Techniques

Coarsely chopped sun-dried tomatoes add an intense tomato flavor and chewy texture to salad.

Combine salad dressing ingredients in a jar; cover tightly, and shake vigorously.

Freshly ground pepper from a hand-held pepper mill adds a sharp, lively flavor to salad dressing.

Artichokes with Orzo Salad

Artichokes with Orzo Salad

½ cup orzo (rice-shaped pasta), uncooked
1 carrot, diced
2 green onions, sliced
8 pitted ripe olives
1 tablespoon chopped fresh basil
⅛ teaspoon salt
⅛ teaspoon pepper
Creamy Lemon Dressing, divided
4 artichokes
Lemon wedge
½ cup water
2 teaspoons lemon juice
2 teaspoons vegetable oil
Garnish: ripe olive slices
Chopped fresh parsley

Cook orzo according to package directions; drain. Rinse with cold water; drain.

Combine orzo and next 6 ingredients, mixing well. Stir in 2 tablespoons Creamy Lemon Dressing. Cover and chill.

Wash artichokes by plunging them up and down in cold water. Cut off stem ends, and trim about ½ inch from top of each artichoke. Remove any loose bottom leaves. With scissors, trim away about one-fourth of each outer leaf. Rub top and edge of leaves with a lemon wedge to prevent discoloration.

Place artichokes upside down in a 2½-quart baking dish. Add ½ cup water, lemon juice, and oil. Cover and microwave at HIGH 14 minutes, giving dish a quarter-turn halfway through cooking time. Let stand, covered, 5 minutes. Plunge into cold water. Drain.

Spread artichoke leaves apart; scrape out fuzzy thistle center (choke) with a spoon. Spoon orzo mixture into cavities. Garnish, if desired.

Serve artichokes with remaining Creamy Lemon Dressing. Sprinkle dressing with parsley.
Yield: 4 servings.

Creamy Lemon Dressing

2 tablespoons lemon juice
2 tablespoons red wine vinegar
1 tablespoon brown mustard
¼ teaspoon garlic powder
2 tablespoons egg substitute
½ cup vegetable oil

Combine first 4 ingredients in container of an electric blender or food processor; process 15 seconds. Add egg substitute, and process 15 seconds. With blender or processor running, gradually add oil, mixing just until well blended. **Yield: ⅔ cup.**

Artichoke-Pasta Salad

2 tablespoons white wine vinegar
2 tablespoons lemon juice
1 teaspoon Dijon mustard
⅓ cup olive oil
¼ cup chopped fresh parsley
2 tablespoons chopped fresh basil
1½ cups orzo (rice-shaped pasta), uncooked
1 (14-ounce) can artichoke hearts, drained and quartered
⅔ cup grated Parmesan cheese
Lettuce leaves
4 ounces prosciutto, cut into ½-inch strips
4 green onions, thinly sliced

Combine first 3 ingredients in container of an electric blender or food processor; process until blended. With blender or processor still running, add oil in a slow, steady stream; process until blended. Stir in parsley and basil. Set dressing aside.

Cook orzo according to package directions; drain. Rinse with cold water; drain.

Combine orzo, artichoke hearts, Parmesan cheese, and dressing; toss gently. Cover and chill.

Arrange orzo mixture on a lettuce-lined platter; sprinkle with prosciutto and green onions.
Yield: 6 servings.

Bow Tie Pasta Primavera

Bow Tie Pasta Primavera

8 ounces bow tie pasta, uncooked
2 tablespoons olive oil, divided
3 green onions, cut into 1-inch pieces
2 cloves garlic, minced
½ pound fresh asparagus
2 cups broccoli flowerets
1 (10-ounce) package frozen English peas,
    thawed and drained
½ pound fresh mushrooms, sliced
1 small tomato, finely chopped
1 small sweet red pepper, seeded and chopped
1 cup freshly grated Parmesan cheese
¼ cup minced fresh parsley
¼ cup white wine vinegar
¼ cup olive oil
½ teaspoon salt
½ teaspoon dried oregano
½ teaspoon dried basil
½ teaspoon dried thyme
¼ teaspoon black pepper
⅛ teaspoon ground red pepper

Cook pasta according to package directions; drain. Rinse with cold water; drain. Place pasta in a large serving bowl; toss with 1 tablespoon olive oil.

Cook green onions and garlic in 1 tablespoon hot olive oil in a large skillet over medium-high heat, stirring constantly, until crisp-tender; add to pasta, tossing gently.

Snap off tough ends of asparagus. Remove scales with a vegetable peeler or knife, if desired. Cut asparagus into 1-inch pieces.

Arrange asparagus and broccoli in a vegetable steamer over boiling water; cover and steam 4 minutes or until crisp-tender.

Add asparagus mixture, peas, and remaining ingredients to pasta mixture; toss gently. Cover and chill 3 to 4 hours, tossing occasionally. **Yield: 8 servings.**

Confetti Orzo Salad

1½ cups orzo (rice-shaped pasta), uncooked
1 carrot, scraped and chopped
1¼ cups chopped sweet red, green, or yellow
    pepper
½ cup peeled, seeded, and chopped cucumber
¼ cup thinly sliced green onions
¼ cup chopped purple onion
¼ cup chopped fresh parsley
2 tablespoons white wine vinegar
½ teaspoon grated lemon rind
3 tablespoons lemon juice
¾ teaspoon salt
⅛ teaspoon coarsely ground pepper
2 cloves garlic, minced
⅓ cup olive oil

Cook orzo according to package directions; drain. Rinse with cold water; drain.

Combine orzo, carrot, and next 5 ingredients; set aside.

Combine vinegar and next 5 ingredients. Gradually add oil, beating with a wire whisk until blended. Pour over orzo mixture, tossing gently. Cover and chill. **Yield: 8 to 10 servings.**

Ramen Noodle Salad

2 cups water
1 (3-ounce) package chicken-flavored Ramen
     noodles
1 teaspoon butter
¼ cup finely chopped celery
¼ cup shredded carrot
¼ cup thinly sliced green onions
1 tablespoon finely chopped green pepper
1 teaspoon lemon juice
1 teaspoon soy sauce
2 tablespoons mayonnaise

Bring water to a boil. Crumble noodles, and add to water; stir in seasoning packet. Return to a boil, and cook 2 minutes, stirring often. Drain.

Combine noodles and butter, stirring until butter melts. Add celery and remaining ingredients, stirring gently to coat. Cover and chill 3 to 4 hours. **Yield: 2 servings.**

Vegetable Pasta Salad

8 ounces rotini (corkscrew pasta), uncooked
1 teaspoon salt
1 medium onion, chopped
1 cup sliced fresh mushrooms
1 clove garlic, minced
2 tablespoons olive oil
1 medium carrot, thinly sliced
1 cup broccoli flowerets
1 medium zucchini, thinly sliced
1 cup frozen English peas
2 tablespoons chopped fresh basil or
     2 teaspoons dried basil
2 tablespoons chopped fresh parsley
1 pint cherry tomatoes, cut in half
Vinaigrette Dressing
Lettuce leaves
Garnish: grated Parmesan cheese

Cook pasta according to package directions, using 1 teaspoon salt; drain. Rinse with cold water; drain. Set aside.

Cook onion, mushrooms, and garlic in 2 tablespoons olive oil in a Dutch oven, stirring constantly, until onion is tender. Add carrot, broccoli, zucchini, and peas; cook 2 minutes.

Add pasta, basil, and parsley to Dutch oven, mixing well. Stir in tomatoes.

Toss pasta mixture with Vinaigrette Dressing, and serve on lettuce leaves. Garnish, if desired. **Yield: 10 to 12 servings.**

Vinaigrette Dressing

⅓ cup olive oil
¼ cup red wine vinegar
1 tablespoon water
1 teaspoon minced onion
1 clove garlic, minced
¼ teaspoon salt
¼ teaspoon sugar
¼ teaspoon paprika
¼ teaspoon pepper
⅛ teaspoon dry mustard

Combine all ingredients in a jar. Cover tightly, and shake vigorously. **Yield: ⅔ cup.**

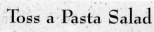

Toss a Pasta Salad

Turn leftover plain pasta into an impromptu pasta salad—simply add chopped raw or cooked vegetables, and toss with your favorite salad dressing. Add diced or shredded cheese and cooked ham, poultry, or seafood for other variations.

Versatile Pasta Salad

4 ounces rotini (corkscrew pasta), uncooked
1 cup sliced fresh mushrooms
1 cup broccoli flowerets
1 cup diced Cheddar cheese
½ cup shredded carrot
½ cup chopped sweet red pepper
¼ teaspoon seasoned salt
¼ teaspoon pepper
⅓ cup vegetable oil
¼ cup white wine vinegar
1 tablespoon Dijon mustard
¼ cup finely chopped green onions
1 tablespoon minced fresh parsley
2 cloves garlic, crushed
½ teaspoon sugar
½ teaspoon dried basil
¼ teaspoon salt
¼ teaspoon dried oregano
¼ teaspoon dried crushed red pepper flakes

Cook rotini according to package directions; drain. Rinse with cold water; drain.

Combine pasta and next 7 ingredients in a large bowl. Set aside.

Combine vegetable oil and next 10 ingredients in a jar. Cover tightly, and shake vigorously. Pour dressing over pasta mixture; toss well.

Chill in a tightly covered container at least 2 hours and up to 3 days. **Yield: 4½ cups.**

Variations

Summer Pasta Salad: Substitute 1 small zucchini, thinly sliced, 1 small yellow squash, thinly sliced, and 6 to 8 cherry tomatoes, halved, for mushrooms and broccoli. **Yield: about 4½ cups.**

Pasta Salad Roma: Substitute 1 (14-ounce) can artichoke hearts, drained and quartered, 1 cup cubed salami, 1 cup diced mozzarella cheese, and ½ cup sliced ripe olives for broccoli, carrot, and Cheddar cheese. **Yield: 4 cups.**

Colorful Pasta Salad

1 pound tri-colored rotini (corkscrew pasta), uncooked
1 green pepper, seeded and chopped
1 sweet red pepper, seeded and chopped
1 (8-ounce) can sliced water chestnuts, drained
1 bunch green onions, chopped
Cherry tomatoes (optional)
¾ cup vegetable oil
¼ cup cider vinegar
1½ teaspoons salt
1½ teaspoons pepper
1 clove garlic, crushed

Cook pasta according to package directions, omitting salt; drain. Rinse with cold water; drain.

Combine pasta, peppers, water chestnuts, green onions and, if desired, cherry tomatoes in a bowl.

Combine oil and next 4 ingredients; mix well. Pour over pasta; toss well. Cover and chill 8 hours, stirring occasionally. **Yield: 12 servings.**

Antipasto Kabobs

1 (9-ounce) package refrigerated cheese-filled tortellini, uncooked
1 (14-ounce) can quartered artichoke hearts, drained
1 (6-ounce) jar pitted ripe olives, drained
½ pound (2-inch-round) thin pepperoni slices
1 (8-ounce) bottle reduced-fat Parmesan Italian salad dressing

Cook tortellini according to package directions, omitting salt. Drain and cool.

Thread tortellini and next 3 ingredients onto 25 (6-inch) wooden skewers. Place in a 13- x 9- x 2-inch dish; drizzle with salad dressing, turning to coat.

Cover and chill at least 4 hours. Drain before serving. **Yield: 10 to 12 appetizer servings.**

Tortellini-Pesto Salad

Tortellini-Pesto Salad

1 (9-ounce) package refrigerated cheese-filled
   tortellini, uncooked
1 small sweet red pepper, cut into thin strips
¾ cup broccoli flowerets
⅓ cup carrot slices
⅓ cup sliced pimiento-stuffed olives
½ cup mayonnaise
¼ cup commercial pesto sauce
¼ cup milk
2 tablespoons grated Parmesan cheese
1 tablespoon olive oil
1 teaspoon white wine vinegar
1 clove garlic, minced
Fresh spinach leaves (optional)

Cook tortellini according to package directions; drain. Rinse with cold water; drain.

Combine tortellini and next 4 ingredients in a medium bowl; set aside.

Combine mayonnaise and next 6 ingredients; spoon over tortellini mixture, and toss gently.

Cover and chill until ready to serve. Serve on fresh spinach leaves, if desired. **Yield: 4 to 6 servings.**

Garden Tortellini Salad

1 (9-ounce) package refrigerated cheese-filled
   tortellini, uncooked
1 (7-ounce) package refrigerated cheese-filled
   spinach tortellini, uncooked
3 cups broccoli flowerets
½ pound carrots, scraped and sliced
2 small green onions, sliced
1 small sweet red pepper, cut into strips
¼ cup finely chopped fresh basil
2 tablespoons egg substitute
1 tablespoon lemon juice
1½ teaspoons Dijon mustard
1½ teaspoons balsamic vinegar
½ cup vegetable oil
¼ cup olive oil
1½ teaspoons grated orange rind
½ teaspoon dried thyme
½ teaspoon salt
⅛ teaspoon ground white pepper

Cook tortellini according to package directions; drain. Rinse with cold water; drain.

Cook broccoli and carrot in a small amount of boiling water 5 minutes or just until crisp-tender; drain well.

Combine tortellini, broccoli, carrot, and next 3 ingredients in a large bowl.

Position knife blade in food processor bowl; add egg substitute and next 3 ingredients. Process 30 seconds. Remove food pusher.

Pour oils slowly through food chute with processor running, blending just until smooth. Add orange rind and next 3 ingredients to dressing; process 30 seconds.

Pour dressing over pasta mixture; toss well. Cover and chill salad at least 2 hours before serving. **Yield: 10 to 12 servings.**

Simmering Sauces

These flavorful sauces don't have to simmer for hours.
You can make most of them in the time it takes to cook the pasta.

Marinara Sauce, Quick Spaghetti and Meat Sauce, Italian Sauce

Quick Spaghetti Sauce, Southwestern Tomato Sauce, Creamy Tomato Sauce

Bow Tie with Marinara, Spinach Pasta Sauce, Baked Ziti, Italian Tomato Sauce

Dried Tomato Spaghetti Sauce, Grilled Chicken-Pasta Salad

Easy Spaghetti Meat Sauce (page 140)

Marinara Sauce

½ cup chopped onion
2 cloves garlic, crushed
1 tablespoon olive oil
4 (14½-ounce) cans tomatoes, drained and
    chopped
2 tablespoons lemon juice
1 tablespoon dried Italian seasoning
2 bay leaves

Cook onion and garlic in olive oil in a Dutch oven over medium-high heat, stirring constantly, until tender. Stir in tomatoes and remaining ingredients.

Bring mixture to a boil; reduce heat to medium, and cook 20 minutes or until most of liquid evaporates, stirring occasionally.

Remove and discard bay leaves. **Yield: 5 cups.**

Quick Spaghetti and Meat Sauce

½ pound ground beef
1½ cups Marinara Sauce (recipe above)
Hot cooked spaghetti or linguine
2 tablespoons grated Parmesan cheese

Brown beef in a skillet, stirring until it crumbles. Drain; return to skillet.

Stir in Marinara Sauce; cook over medium heat 5 minutes. Serve over pasta, and sprinkle with cheese. **Yield: 2 servings.**

Marinara Magic

Make the Marinara Sauce in 30 minutes, and have a head start on other quick meals. You can also use this sauce in any recipe calling for a marinara sauce.

Bow Tie with Marinara

4 to 8 ounces bow tie pasta, uncooked
1 to 2 cups Marinara Sauce (recipe at left)
Freshly grated Parmesan cheese

Cook pasta according to package directions; drain well.

Combine pasta and Marinara Sauce; sprinkle with cheese. **Yield: 2 servings.**

Baked Ziti

1 (16-ounce) package ziti (short tubular
    pasta), uncooked
1 pound mild Italian sausage
½ pound ground beef
½ cup chopped onion
3 cups Marinara Sauce (recipe at left)
1 (16-ounce) package sliced mozzarella cheese
¼ cup grated Parmesan cheese

Cook pasta according to package directions; drain and set aside.

Remove sausage from casing. Cook sausage, beef, and onion in a large skillet over medium heat, stirring until meat crumbles. Drain and return to skillet.

Stir Marinara Sauce and cooked ziti into meat mixture. Layer half each of ziti mixture and mozzarella cheese in a lightly greased 13- x 9- x 2-inch baking dish. Spoon remaining ziti mixture over mozzarella cheese; cover with foil.

Bake at 350° for 15 minutes. Remove foil; add remaining mozzarella cheese, and sprinkle with Parmesan cheese. Bake 10 additional minutes. **Yield: 8 to 10 servings.**

Bow Tie with Marinara

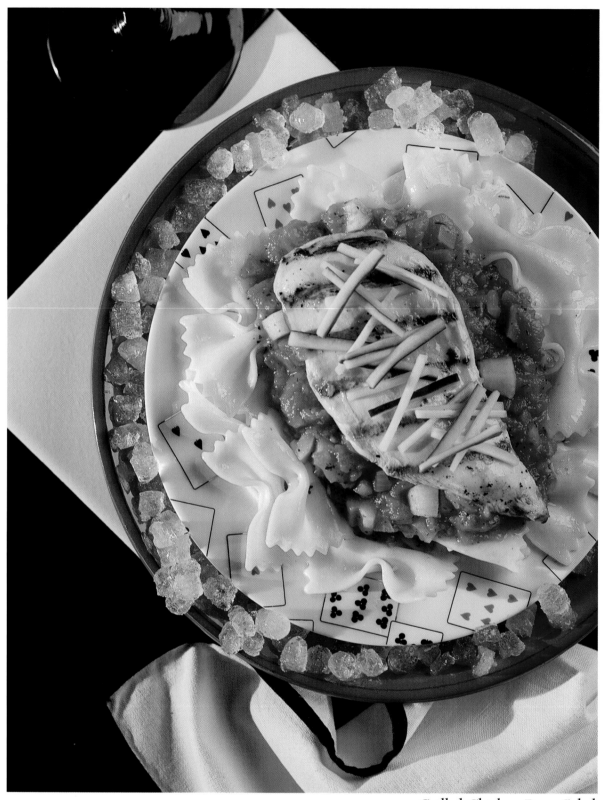

Grilled Chicken-Pasta Salad

Grilled Chicken-Pasta Salad

4 ounces bow tie pasta, uncooked
½ cup Italian salad dressing, divided
2 skinned and boned chicken breast halves
½ small cucumber
1 cup Marinara Sauce, chilled (recipe on
    page 132)

Cook pasta according to package directions, omitting salt; drain.

Combine pasta and 2 tablespoons salad dressing in a bowl, and toss gently. Cover pasta mixture, and chill at least 8 hours.

Place chicken in a shallow dish; drizzle with remaining salad dressing, turning to coat. Cover and chill 2 hours.

Cut cucumber half crosswise into 2 equal portions. Peel and chop 1 portion of cucumber; cut remaining portion into thin strips, and set aside. Stir chopped cucumber into Marinara Sauce, and set aside.

Drain chicken breasts; cook, without grill lid, over hot coals (450° to 500°) for 5 to 7 minutes on each side or until chicken is tender.

Arrange pasta on individual salad plates; spoon sauce over pasta, and top with chicken breasts and cucumber strips. **Yield: 2 servings.**

Italian Tomato Sauce

3 large vine-ripened tomatoes
2 tablespoons extra-virgin olive oil
3 cloves garlic, minced
¼ cup sliced ripe olives
1 tablespoon chopped fresh basil
1 tablespoon chopped fresh parsley
¼ teaspoon salt
¼ teaspoon pepper
4 ounces spaghetti, uncooked
4 ounces mozzarella cheese, cut into cubes

Peel tomatoes; coarsely chop over a medium bowl, reserving juice.

Combine tomato, reserved juice, olive oil, and next 6 ingredients; cover and let stand at room temperature 1 hour.

Cook pasta according to package directions; drain. Serve tomato mixture over pasta, and top with cheese. **Yield: 2 servings.**

Creamy Tomato Sauce

2 cloves garlic, minced
2 tablespoons butter or margarine, melted
6 large tomatoes, peeled, seeded, and chopped
    (about 5 pounds)
½ teaspoon salt
¼ teaspoon freshly ground pepper
½ cup whipping cream
2 tablespoons chopped fresh basil or
    2 teaspoons dried basil
Hot cooked vermicelli

Cook garlic in butter in a large skillet over medium heat, stirring constantly, 1 minute.

Add tomato, salt, and pepper; cook 12 to 15 minutes or until sauce is thickened. Gradually stir in whipping cream and basil, and cook 10 additional minutes.

Serve sauce over vermicelli. **Yield: 4 to 6 servings.**

Dried Tomato Spaghetti Sauce

1 (7-ounce) jar oil-packed dried tomatoes, undrained
1 cup chopped onion
1 cup chopped celery
1 cup diced carrot
3 cloves garlic, minced
2 (28-ounce) cans whole tomatoes, undrained
⅔ cup dry white wine
1 teaspoon dried fennel seeds
½ teaspoon pepper

Drain dried tomatoes, reserving ¼ cup oil. Chop tomatoes; set aside.

Heat reserved oil in a Dutch oven; cook onion, celery, carrot, and garlic in hot oil 15 minutes, stirring occasionally.

Stir in dried and canned tomatoes, wine, fennel seeds, and pepper; cook, uncovered, over medium heat 1 hour or to desired consistency, stirring occasionally.

Position knife blade in food processor bowl; add half of sauce mixture. Pulse 4 or 5 times or until mixture is chopped but not smooth. Repeat procedure with remaining half of sauce mixture. Serve over hot pasta. **Yield: 6 cups.**

Spinach Pasta Sauce

2 cloves garlic, sliced
2 tablespoons butter or margarine, melted
2 (9.5-ounce) packages frozen creamed spinach, thawed
1 cup half-and-half
⅓ cup grated Parmesan cheese
Hot cooked spaghetti
4 slices bacon, cooked and crumbled

Cook garlic in butter in a medium saucepan over medium heat, stirring constantly, until lightly browned; remove and discard garlic.

Add spinach and half-and-half to butter. Bring to a boil, stirring constantly; reduce heat, and add Parmesan cheese. Cook over low heat, stirring occasionally, 8 to 10 minutes.

Serve sauce over spaghetti; sprinkle with bacon. **Yield: 4 to 6 servings.**

Southwestern Tomato Sauce

3 small vine-ripened tomatoes
2 tablespoons extra-virgin olive oil
3 cloves garlic, minced
1 jalapeño pepper, seeded and finely chopped
3 tablespoons chopped fresh cilantro
1 tablespoon fresh lime juice
½ teaspoon chili powder
¼ teaspoon salt
¼ teaspoon ground white pepper
4 ounces angel hair pasta, uncooked
4 ounces goat cheese, crumbled
2 tablespoons pine nuts, toasted

Peel tomatoes, and coarsely chop over a medium bowl, reserving juice.

Combine chopped tomato, reserved juice, olive oil, and next 7 ingredients; cover and let stand at room temperature 1 hour.

Cook pasta according to package directions; drain. Serve tomato mixture over pasta; top with cheese and pine nuts. **Yield: 2 servings.**

Try Sun-Dried Tomatoes

Sun-dried tomatoes add a rich, robust flavor to pasta dishes—especially sauces, salads, and entrées. They come packed either dry or in olive oil. Recipes usually suggest that the dry-pack type be soaked in water or cooked in a liquid before use.

Southwestern Tomato Sauce

Quick Spaghetti Sauce

Quick Spaghetti Sauce

3⅓ cups Ground Beef Mix
1 (28-ounce) can crushed tomatoes, undrained
½ cup water
¼ cup tomato paste
¼ cup chopped fresh parsley
1 bay leaf
½ teaspoon dried basil
½ teaspoon dried oregano
¼ to ½ teaspoon salt
¼ teaspoon dried thyme
¼ teaspoon pepper
Hot cooked spaghetti

Heat Ground Beef Mix, or cook frozen Ground Beef Mix in a 3-quart saucepan over medium heat until thoroughly heated. Add crushed tomatoes and next 9 ingredients; stir well.

Bring mixture to a boil; reduce heat, and simmer 20 minutes, stirring occasionally. Remove and discard bay leaf. Serve sauce over hot cooked spaghetti. **Yield: 6 cups.**

Ground Beef Mix

3 pounds ground beef
1 large green pepper, finely chopped
3 cloves garlic, minced
1 cup water
1 tablespoon plus 1 teaspoon beef-flavored bouillon granules
2 medium onions, finely chopped
¼ teaspoon pepper

Cook beef, green pepper, and garlic in a large skillet over medium-high heat until meat browns and crumbles. Remove from skillet, and drain well.

Add water and bouillon granules to skillet. Bring to a boil, stirring to dissolve granules.

Add onion; cover, reduce heat to medium, and cook 15 minutes. Uncover and cook 5 to 10 minutes or until liquid evaporates. Stir onion mixture and pepper into beef mixture. **Yield: 10 cups.**

Note: To freeze Ground Beef Mix, spread mixture in a 15- x 10- x 1-inch jellyroll pan; cool. Cover tightly, and freeze at least 4 hours. Crumble frozen mixture into small pieces. Freeze in 3 (1-quart) labeled airtight containers up to 2 months.

Italian Sauce

2 pounds ground beef
1½ cups chopped onion
1 clove garlic, chopped
2 (16-ounce) cans plum tomatoes, undrained and chopped
1 (6-ounce) can tomato paste
1 cup water
2 tablespoons chopped fresh parsley or 2 teaspoons dried parsley flakes
1 tablespoon sugar
1½ teaspoons salt
1 teaspoon dried oregano
1 teaspoon dried basil
½ teaspoon pepper

Cook first 3 ingredients in a large skillet over medium heat, stirring until meat browns and crumbles; drain well. Stir in tomatoes and remaining ingredients.

Bring to a boil over medium heat, stirring occasionally. Reduce heat, and simmer, uncovered, 45 minutes. Serve sauce with spaghetti, lasagna, or manicotti. **Yield: 7½ cups.**

Note: To freeze, prepare recipe as directed, and freeze in 2 (1½-quart) airtight containers or freezer bags up to 2 months.

To defrost and reheat: For **conventional** method, thaw sauce in refrigerator, and cook in saucepan 15 minutes or until thoroughly heated. For **microwave** oven, cover and defrost one container of sauce in a 1½-quart baking dish at MEDIUM (50% power) 20 minutes, rotating dish after 10 minutes. Microwave at HIGH 5 minutes or until thoroughly heated, stirring after 3 minutes.

Easy Spaghetti Meat Sauce

(pictured on page 131)

Servings				Ingredients
For 8	**For 16**	**For 24**	**For 32**	
2 lbs	4 lbs	6 lbs	8 lbs	**Ground beef**
1	2	3	4	**15-ounce can(s) tomato sauce**
2 cups	3 cups	4 cups	5 cups	**Water**
¼ cup	½ cup	¾ cup	1 cup	**Dried onion flakes**
1½ Tbsp	3 Tbsp	¼ cup	⅓ cup	**Worcestershire sauce**
1 tsp	2 tsp	1 Tbsp	1½ Tbsp	**Garlic powder**
½ tsp	1 tsp	1½ tsp	2 tsp	**Pepper**
1	2	3	4	**28-ounce jar(s) spaghetti sauce**
1	2	3	4	**16-ounce package(s) spaghetti, uncooked**
				Grated Parmesan cheese

To serve 24, prepare sauce in an 8-quart Dutch oven.

To serve 32 without the use of institutional cooking equipment, divide the ingredients in half, and cook in 2 Dutch ovens.

Brown ground beef in a large Dutch oven, stirring until beef crumbles and draining once during browning. Drain beef again. Stir in tomato sauce and next 5 ingredients.

Bring to a boil over medium heat. Cover, reduce heat, and simmer 20 minutes, stirring occasionally. Add spaghetti sauce; simmer, uncovered, 20 minutes, stirring occasionally.

Cook spaghetti according to package directions; drain. Spoon meat sauce over cooked spaghetti, and sprinkle with Parmesan cheese.

Note: To make ahead, freeze sauce in an airtight container up to 2 months; thaw in refrigerator. To prepare spaghetti ahead, cook pasta; drain and chill. To reheat cooked pasta, place in a colander, and immerse in boiling water for 1 to 2 minutes; drain. Or microwave at HIGH, stirring occasionally, until pasta is just heated through.

Match Pasta with a Sauce

- Thin sauces, such as marinara sauce or pesto sauce, should be served with thin pasta.
- Thicker, chunkier meat and vegetable sauces go well with tubular and shell pastas that are designed to "trap" the toppings.
- Chunky vegetable or meat sauces should be served with thick pasta: ziti, mostaccioli, rigatoni, or fettuccine.
- Rich, thick, smooth sauces need a flat pasta that won't trap too much of the sauce.

Index